No Substitute for Madness

Ron Jones

A Teacher, His Kids & The Lessons of Real Life

Illustrations by Tom Parker

Island Press   Covelo, California

Printed in the United States of America

Library of Congress Cataloging in Publication Data
Jones, Ron, 1941–
1. Teacher-student relationships—United States. 2. Jones, Ron,
1941– 3. High School teachers—United States—Biography. I. Title.
LB1033.J66   373.11'02   80-28308
ISBN 0-933280-06-8

Special thanks to Toni Burbank and Bantam Books for permission to
include "The Acorn People" in this book. Thanks also to Tom Parker
for the illustrations, Jeremy Hewes for editing, and Georgia Oliva for
design.

Portions of this book have previously appeared, in different form, in
CoEvolution Quarterly, *Psychology Today*, *Media & Methods*, *Reader's Digest*, *Scholastic Scope*, *Learning*, *EastWest Journal*, and *The Sun*.

Contents

Introduction   v

The Third Wave   1

The Acorn People   25

Winning   69

There Is No School on the Sixth Floor   87

The High Diving Board   101

The Last Meeting   111

We Killed Them   137

For Deanna

Ron Jones doesn't think of himself as a writer. He is a teacher, and in the course of his work, stories simply happen to him. The "stories" in this book are all true; they happened to Ron Jones during the twenty years he has been a teacher, coach, and camp counselor. Like many other people for whom writing is also learning, Ron initially began to put his experiences down on paper as a way of clarifying them, of coming to grips with the changes that these events made in him and in everyone who was a part of them.

This approach to writing is not new or spectacular; it is the stuff of journals and memoirs aplenty. What makes these stories compelling is the events that they portray and the elemental way in which Ron Jones's words communicate. Throughout *No Substitute for Madness,* he speaks from the heart, telling in direct, staccato prose how he felt as he struggled to move a child's limp body from a wheelchair to a toilet seat, or how his class reacted when they learned that their secret society was a sham. The events that provoke these feelings are an experiment in Nazi training in a high school class; a collection of severely handicapped children trying to cope with two weeks in a camp built for Boy Scouts, not wheelchairs; and a group of streetwise teenagers teaching adolescent mental patients about life outside the hospital. Through these and other episodes from his teaching career, Ron Jones has illuminated some of life's profound lessons.

Ron does have a particular way of looking at the world, and that perspective is evident in *No Substitute for Madness.* In each of this book's chapters, a group of young people and their teacher (or coach or counselor) must contend with issues that are thrust upon them from the world at large—the borrowed Boy Scout camp, with stairs where ramps are needed; the official whimsy of a basketball league that invites black players from another school, then declares them ineligible to play; the school board and administrators who refuse to acknowledge a campus political club or to recognize the deep divisions within their own community. These forces rub against each other like sandpaper: somehow the teacher and kids must confront real life and keep their integrity and hope intact. Most of the time, in Ron Jones's experience, somehow they do.

In addition to its basis in fact, *No Substitute for Madness* has a lively history as literature. When Ron wrote the first accounts of his teaching experience, in 1976, he published six stories in a typewriter-on-newsprint book, which was the original version of *No Substitute for Madness*. Three of those early stories are included here: "The Third Wave," "Winning," and "The Last Meeting." Within a year, Ron had distributed all 3000 copies of this small book, mainly through Zephyros Education Exchange, a network of teachers that he founded. He also sent "The Third Wave" and "Winning" to several magazines and—uncharacteristically, for the publishing business—got them to agree to nonexclusive use of the stories.

Through Ron's efforts as a fledgling publisher, "The Third Wave" became news. The mid-1970s had seen a noisy revival of the American Nazi Party in some cities, and here was a true account of a high school history class that had tried out a week of Nazi-like authoritarian discipline and indoctrination. Ron was interviewed by local reporters for radio, TV, and newspapers, and a wire service story about his teaching experiment ran in papers across the country. He was invited to appear on "Good Morning America," and two associates of Norman Lear saw that interview and suggested that Lear buy the dramatic rights to

Ron's story. (Lear did buy the story, and it has been tentatively scheduled as a television special in the spring of 1981.

"The Third Wave" also gained international attention. The story was reprinted in the prestigious German magazine *Der Speigel,* and one German television station sent a crew to San Francisco to interview Ron and some of his former students about the episode, even though it had taken place a decade before.

In 1977, Ron wrote and published "The Acorn People," which he distributed to the Zephyros network and sent to a number of book reviewers and magazines. The response was immediate to this touching account of handicapped kids who become mountain climbers, pirates, and kings at a summer camp. The complete story was published in *CoEvolution Quarterly,* and abridged versions have appeared in *Psychology Today, Media & Methods,* and *Reader's Digest.*

Because of the enthusiastic reviews and word-of-mouth publicity for "The Acorn People," Jones's 5000 self-published copies were sold within a few months, without benefit of any traditional book distribution network. Then Bantam Books purchased the story, and their paperback version has sold steadily to a school market. In addition, Abingdon, a religious publisher, issued a hard-cover edition of this book.

A film adaptation of "The Acorn People" also seemed inevitable. Although the project has been several years in the making, NBC Television is scheduled to show a film of "The Acorn People" in February 1981, starring Lavar Burton, Cloris Leachman, and Ted Bessel. This television movie was written and directed by Joan Tewkesbury.

Another of the stories in this collection, "There Is No School on the Sixth Floor," recounts the summer school program that Ron Jones set up to give jobs to college-age young people and to introduce the teenage residents of a mental hospital to the world beyond their institution. This story has been published in several magazines, and it became the basis for a much longer account that Ron has written about his work at this hospital. (This longer version is slated for future publication by Bantam under the title *Kids Called Crazy*.)

The remaining two stories in this updated version of *No Substitute for Madness* are new. "The High Diving Board" is a sort of meditation, a brief interlude in which the writer observes youth and age and accomplishment. "We Killed Them" brings us up to date with Ron's teaching career. As director of physical education at the Recreation Center for the Handicapped in San Francisco, Ron recently coached a basketball team that went to the statewide Special Olympics tournament. "We Killed Them" is his account of that trip and of the rich surprises in this weekend of comrades and competition.

Surprises, in fact, are at the heart of this teacher's work. For Ron Jones, surprises are the gifts of being alive, and his writing shares discoveries in stories that tap our reservoirs of feeling and knowing. Quite simply, Ron Jones is attuned to the special music of humanity, and his words play magnificent variations on this welcome theme.

Jeremy Joan Hewes
San Francisco, November 1980

The Third Wave

For years I kept a strange secret. I shared this silence with 200 students. Yesterday I ran into one of those students, and it all rushed back.

Steve Coniglio had been a sophomore in my World History class. We ran into each other quite by accident. It's one of those occasions experienced by teachers when they least expect it. You're walking down the street, eating at a secluded restaurant, or buying some underwear, when all of a sudden an ex-student pops up to say hello. In this case it was Steve, running down the street shouting, "Mr. Jones! Mr. Jones!" We greeted with an embarrassed hug.

I had to stop for a minute to remember. Who is this young man hugging me? He calls me Mr. Jones. Must be a former student. What's his name?

In the split second of my race back in time, Steve sensed my questioning and backed up. Then he smiled, and slowly raised a hand in a cupped position.

My God. He's a member of the Third Wave. It's Steve, Steve Coniglio. He sat in the second row. He was a sensitive and bright student. Played guitar and enjoyed drama.

We just stood there exchanging smiles when, without

a conscious command, I raised my hand in curved position; the salute was given. Two comrades had met long after the war. The Third Wave was still alive.

"Mr. Jones, do you remember the Third Wave?"

I sure do. It was one of the most frightening events I ever experienced in the classroom. It was also the genesis of a secret that I and 200 students would share for the rest of our lives.

We talked about the Third Wave for the next few hours. Then it was time to part. It's strange, you meet a past student in these chance ways. You catch a few moments of your life. Hold them tight. Then say goodbye, not knowing when and if you'll ever see each other again. Oh, you make promises to call each other, but it won't happen. Steve will continue to grow and change. I will remain an ageless benchmark in his life—a presence that will not change. I am Mr. Jones. Steve turns and gives a silent salute, his hand raised upward in a shape of a curling wave. Hand curved in a similar fashion, I return the gesture.

The Third Wave. Well, at last it can be talked about. Here I've met a student and we've talked for hours about this nightmare. The secret must finally be waning. It's taken a dozen years. It's now just a dream, something to remember—no, it's something we tried to forget. That's how it all started. By strange coincidence, I think it was Steve who started the Third Wave with a question.

We were studying Nazi Germany and, in the middle of a lecture, I was interrupted by the question. How could the German populace claim ignorance of the slaughter of the Jewish people? How could the townspeople—railroad conductors, teachers, doctors—claim that they knew nothing about concentration camps and human carnage? How could people who were neighbors and maybe even friends of the Jewish citizens say they weren't there when it happened? It was a good question. I didn't know the answer.

Inasmuch as there were several months still to go in the school year and I was already at World War II, I decided to take a week and explore the question.

STRENGTH THROUGH DISCIPLINE

On Monday, I introduced my sophomore history students to one of the experiences that characterized Nazi Germany. Discipline. I lectured about the beauty of discipline. How an athlete feels having worked hard and regularly to be successful at a sport. How a ballet dancer or painter works hard to perfect a movement. The dedicated patience of a scientist in pursuit of an idea. It's discipline. That self-training. Control. The power of the will. The exchange of physical hardships for superior mental and physical facilities. The ultimate triumph.

To experience the power of discipline, I invited, no, I commanded the class to exercise and use a new seating posture; I described how proper sitting posture assists concentration and strengthens the will. In fact, I instructed the class in a mandatory sitting posture. This posture started with feet flat on the floor, hands placed flat across the small of the back to force a straight alignment of the spine. "There—can't you breathe more easily? You're more alert. Don't you feel better?"

We practiced this new attention position over and over. I walked up and down the aisles of seated students pointing out small flaws, making improvements. Proper seating became the most important aspect of learning. I would dismiss the class, allowing them to leave their desks, and then call them abruptly back to an attention sitting position. In speed drills the class learned to move from standing position to attention sitting in fifteen seconds. In focus drills I concentrated attention on the feet being parallel and flat, ankles locked, knees bent at ninety-degree angles, hands flat and crossed against the back, spine straight, chin down, head forward. We did noise drills in which talking was allowed only to be shown as a detraction. Following minutes of progressive drill assignments the class could move from standing positions outside the room to attention sitting positions at their desks without making a sound. The maneuver took five seconds.

It was strange how quickly the students took to this uniform code of behavior. I began to wonder just how far they could be pushed. Was this display of obedience a momentary game we were all playing, or was it something else? Was the desire for discipline and uniformity a natural need—a societal instinct we hide within our franchise restaurants and TV programming?

I decided to push the tolerance of the class for regimented action. In the final twenty-five minutes of the class I introduced some new rules. Students must be sitting in class at the attention position before the late bell; all students must carry pencils and paper for note taking; when asking or answering questions students must stand at the side of their desks; and the first word given in answering or asking a question must be "Mr. Jones."

Students who responded to questions in a sluggish manner were reprimanded and in every case made to repeat their behavior until it was a model of punctuality and respect. The intensity of the response became more important than the content. To accentuate this, I requested that answers be given in three words or less. Students were rewarded for making an effort at answering questions. They were also acknowledged for doing this in a crisp and attentive manner. Soon everyone in the class began popping up with answers and questions. The involvement level in the class moved from the few who always dominated discussions to the entire class. Even stranger was the gradual improvement in the quality of answers. Everyone seemed to be listening more intently. New people were speaking. Answers started to stretch out as students who were usually hesitant to speak found support for their efforts.

As for my part in this exercise, I had nothing but questions. Why hadn't I thought of this technique before? Students seemed intent on the assignment and displayed accurate recitation of facts and concepts. They even seemed to be asking better questions and treating each other with more compassion. How could this be? Here I was enacting an authoritarian learning environment and it seemed very productive. I began to ponder not just how far this class could be pushed, but how much I would change my basic beliefs toward an open classroom and self-directed learning. Was all my belief in Carl Rogers to shrivel and die? Where was this experiment leading?

STRENGTH THROUGH COMMUNITY

On Tuesday, the second day of the exercise, I entered the classroom to find everyone sitting in silence at the attention position. Some of their faces were relaxed with smiles that come from pleasing the teacher. But most of the students looked straight ahead in earnest concentration. Neck muscles rigid. No sign of a smile or a thought or even a question. Every fiber strained to perform the deed. To release the tension, I went to the chalkboard and wrote in big letters: STRENGTH THROUGH DISCIPLINE. Below this I wrote a second law: STRENGTH THROUGH COMMUNITY.

While the class sat in stern silence I began to talk, lecture, sermonize about the value of community. At this stage of the game I was debating in my own mind whether to stop the experiment or to continue. I hadn't planned such intensity or compliance. In fact, I was surprised to find the ideas on discipline enacted at all. While pondering whether to stop or go on with the experiment, I talked on and on about community. I made up stories from my experiences as an athlete, coach, and historian. It was easy. Community is that bond between individuals who work and struggle together. It's raising a barn with your neighbors, it's feeling that you are a part of something beyond yourself—a movement, a team, La Raza, a cause.

It was too late to step back. I now can appreciate why the astronomer turns relentlessly to the telescope. I was probing deeper and deeper into my own perceptions and the motivations for group and individual action. There was much more to see and try to understand. Many questions haunted me. Why did the students accept the authority I was imposing? Where was their curiosity or resistance to this martial behavior? When and how would this end?

Following my description of community, I once again told the class that community—like discipline—must be experienced if it is to be understood. To provide an encounter with community I had the class recite in unison: "Strength through discipline"; "Strength through community." First I would have two students stand and call out our motto. Then I'd add two more, and two more, until finally the whole class was standing and reciting.

It was fun. The students began to look at each other and sense the power of belonging. Everyone was capable and equal. They were doing something together. We worked on this simple act for the entire class period. We would repeat the mottoes in a rotating chorus, or say them with various degrees of loudness. Always we said them together, emphasizing the proper way to sit, stand, and talk.

I began to think of myself as a part of the experiment. I enjoyed the unified action demonstrated by the students. It was rewarding to see their satisfaction and excitement to do more. I found it harder and harder to extract myself from the momentum and identity that the class was developing. I was following the group dictate as much as I was directing it.

As the class period was ending, and without forethought, I created a class salute. It was for class members only. To make the salute you brought your right hand up toward the right shoulder in a curled position. I called it the Third Wave salute because the hand resembled a wave about to top over. The idea for the three came from beach lore that waves travel in chains, the third wave being the last and largest of each series. Since we had a salute, I made it a rule to salute all class members outside the classroom. When the bell sounded, ending the period, I asked the class for complete silence. With everyone sitting at attention I slowly raised my arm and, with a cupped hand, I saluted. It was a silent signal of recognition. They were something special. Without command the entire group of students returned the salute.

Throughout the next few days students in the class would exchange this greeting. You would be walking down the hall when all of a sudden three classmates would turn your way, each flashing a quick salute. In the library or in gym students would be seen giving this strange hand jive. You would hear a crash of cafeteria food, only to have it followed by two classmates saluting each other. The mystique of thirty individuals doing this strange gyration soon brought more attention to the class and its experiment into the Nazi personality. Many students outside the class asked if they could join.

Strength Through Action

On Wednesday, I decided to issue membership cards to every student who wanted to continue what I now called the experiment. Not a single student elected to leave the room. In this, the third day of activity, there were forty-three students in the class. Thirteen students had cut some other class to be a part of the experiment. While the class sat at attention, I gave each person a card. I marked three of the cards with a red X and informed the recipients that they had a special assignment to report any students not complying with class rules.

I then proceeded to talk about the meaning of action. I discussed the beauty of taking full responsibility for one's actions. Of believing so thoroughly in yourself and your community or family that you will do anything to preserve, protect, and extend that being. I stressed how hard work and allegiance to each other would allow accelerated learning and accomplishment. I reminded students of what it felt like to be in classes where competition caused pain and degradation—situations in which students were pitted against each other in everything from gym to reading. The feeling of never acting, never being a part of something, never supporting each other.

At this point students stood without prompting and began to give what amounted to testimonials.

"Mr. Jones, for the first time I'm learning lots of things."

"Mr. Jones, why don't you teach like this all the time?"

I was shocked! Yes, I had been pushing information

at them in an extremely controlled setting, but the fact that they found it comfortable and acceptable was startling. It was equally disconcerting to realize that complex and time-consuming written homework assignments on German life were being completed and even expanded by students. Performance in academic skill areas was improving significantly. They were learning more. And they seemed to want more. I began to think that the students might do anything I assigned. I decided to find out.

To allow students the experience of direct action, I gave each individual a specific verbal assignment.

"It's your task to design a Third Wave banner."

"You are responsible for stopping any student who is not a Third Wave member from entering this room."

"I want you to remember and be able to recite by tomorrow the name and address of every Third Wave member."

"You are assigned the problem of training and convincing at least twenty children in the adjacent elementary school that our sitting posture is necessary for better learning."

"It's your job to read this pamphlet and report its entire content to the class before the period ends."

"I want each of you to give me the name and address of one reliable friend who you think might want to join the Third Wave."

To conclude the session on direct action, I instructed students in a simple procedure for initiating new members. It went like this. A new member had only to be recommended by an existing member and issued a card by me. Upon receiving this card the new member had to demonstrate knowledge of our rules and pledge obedience to them. My announcement unleashed a fervor.

The school was alive with conjecture and curiosity. It affected everyone. The school cook asked what a Third Wave cookie looked like. I said chocolate chip, of course. Our principal came into an afternoon faculty meeting and gave me the Third Wave salute. I saluted back. The librarian thanked me for the thirty-foot banner on learning, which she placed above the library entrance. By the end of the day more than 200 students were admitted into the order. I felt very alone and a little scared.

Most of my fear emanated from the incidence of tattletaling. Although I formally appointed only three students to report deviant behavior, approximately twenty students came to me with reports about how Allan didn't salute, or Georgene was talking critically about our experiment. This incidence of monitoring meant that half the class now considered it their duty to observe and report on members of their class. Within this avalanche of reporting, one legitimate conspiracy did seem to be under way.

Three women in the class had told their parents all about our classroom activities. These young women were by far the most intelligent students in the class. As friends, they chummed together. They possessed a silent confidence and took pleasure in a school setting that gave them academic and leadership opportunity. During the days of the experiment I was curious about how they would respond to the egalitarian and physical reshaping of the class. The rewards they were accustomed to winning just didn't exist in the experiment. The intellectual skills of questioning and reasoning were nonexistent. In the martial atmosphere of the class they seemed stunned and pensive. Now that I look back, they appeared much like the child with a so-called learning disability. They watched the activities and participated in a mechanical fashion. Others jumped in, whereas they held back, watching.

In telling their parents of the experiment, I set off a brief chain of events. The rabbi for one of the parents called me at home. He was polite and condescending. I told him we were merely studying the Nazi personality. He seemed delighted and told me not to worry; he would talk to the parents and calm their concerns. In concluding this conversation, I envisioned similar conversations throughout history in which the clergy accepted and apologized for untenable conditions. If only he would have raged in anger or simply investigated the situation, I could point the students to an example of righteous rebellion. But no—the rabbi became a part of the experiment. In remaining ignorant of the oppression in the experiment, he became an accomplice and advocate.

By the end of the third day I was exhausted. I was tearing apart. The balance between role-playing and directed behavior became indistinguishable. Many of the students were completely into being Third Wave members. They demanded strict obedience of the rules from other students and bullied those who took the experiment lightly. Others simply sunk into the activity and took self-assigned roles.

I particularly remember Robert. Robert was big for his age and displayed very few academic skills. Oh, he tried harder than anyone I know to be successful. He handed in elaborate weekly reports copied word for word from the reference books in the library. Robert is like so many kids in school who don't excel or cause trouble. They aren't bright, they can't make athletic teams, and they don't strike out for attention. They are lost, invisible. The only reason I came to know Robert at all is that I found him eating lunch in my classroom. He always ate lunch alone.

Well, the Third Wave gave Robert a place in school. At least he was equal to everyone. He could do something.

Take part, be meaningful. That's just what Robert did. Late Wednesday afternoon I found Robert following me and asked what in the world was he doing.

He smiled—I don't think I had ever seen him smile—and announced, "Mr. Jones, I'm your bodyguard. I'm afraid something will happen to you. Can I do it, Mr. Jones? Please?"

Given that assurance and smile, I couldn't say no. I had a bodyguard. All day long Robert opened and closed doors for me. He always walked on my right, smiling and saluting other class members. He followed me everywhere. In the faculty room (closed to students) he stood at silent attention while I gulped some coffee. When an English teacher reminded him that students weren't permitted in the "teachers' room," he just smiled and informed the faculty member that he wasn't a student, he was a bodyguard.

STRENGTH THROUGH PRIDE

On Thursday I began to draw the experiment to a conclusion. I was exhausted and worried. Many students were over the line. The Third Wave had become the center of their existence. I was in pretty bad shape myself. I was now acting instinctively as a dictator. Oh, I was benevolent. And I daily argued to myself on the benefits of the learning experience.

By this, the fourth day of the experiment, I was beginning to lose my own arguments. As I spent more time playing the role, I had less time to remember its rational origins and purpose. I found myself sliding into the role even when it wasn't necessary. I wondered if this doesn't happen to lots of people. We get or take an ascribed role and then bend our life to fit the image. Soon the image is the only identity people will accept. So we become the image. The trouble with the situation and role I had created was that I didn't have time to think where it was leading. Events were crushing around me. I worried for students doing things they would regret. I worried for myself.

Once again I faced the thoughts of closing the experiment or letting it go its own course. Both options were unworkable. If I stopped the experiment a great number of students would be left hanging. They had committed themselves in front of their peers to radical behavior. Emotionally and psychologically they had exposed themselves. If I suddenly jolted them back to classroom reality, I would face a confused student body for the remainder of the year. It would be too painful and demeaning for Robert and the students like him to be twisted back into their seats and told it's just a game. They would take the ridicule from the brighter students who had participated in a measured and cautious way. I couldn't let the Roberts lose again.

The other option—letting the experiment run its course—was also out of the question. Things were already getting out of control. Wednesday evening someone had broken into the room and ransacked the place. I later found out it was the father of one of the students. He was a retired Air Force colonel who had spent time in a German prisoner-of-war camp. Upon hearing of our activity he simply lost control. Late in the evening he broke into the room and tore it apart. I found him propped up against the classroom door the next morning. He told me about his friends who had been killed in Germany. He was holding on to me and shaking. In staccato words he pleaded that I understand and help him get home. I called his wife and, with the help of a neighbor, walked him home. Later we spent hours talking about what he felt and did, but from that moment on Thursday morning I was more concerned with what might be happening at school.

I was increasingly worried about how our activity

was affecting the faculty and other students in the school. The Third Wave was disrupting normal learning. Students were cutting class to participate and the school counselors were beginning to question every student in the class. The real gestapo in the school was at work. Faced with this experiment exploding in a hundred directions, I decided to try an old basketball strategy. When you're playing against all the odds, the best action to take is to try the unexpected. That's what I did.

By Thursday the class had swollen in size to more than eighty students. The only thing that allowed them all to fit was the enforced discipline of sitting in silence at attention. A strange calm is in effect when a room full of people sit in quiet observation and anticipation. It helped me approach them in a deliberate way. I talked about pride. "Pride is more than banners or salutes. Pride is something no one can take from you. Pride is knowing you are the best. . . . It can't be destroyed. . . ."

In the midst of this crescendo I abruptly changed and lowered my voice to announce the real reason for the Third Wave. In a slow, methodic tone I explained: "The Third Wave isn't just an experiment or classroom activity. It's far more important than that. The Third Wave is a nationwide program to find students who are willing to fight for political change in this country. That's right. This activity we have been doing has been practice for the real thing. Across the country teachers like myself have been recruiting and training a youth brigade capable of showing the nation a better society through discipline, community, pride, and action. If we can change the way the school is run, we can change the way that factories, stores, universities, and all the other institutions are run. You are a selected group of young people chosen to help in this cause. If you will stand up and display what you have learned in the past four days, we can change the destiny of this nation. We can bring it a new sense of order, community, pride, and action. A new purpose. Everything rests with you and your willingness to take a stand."

To validate the seriousness of my words I turned to the three women in the class whom I knew had questioned the Third Wave. I demanded that they leave the room. I explained why I acted and then assigned four guards to escort the women to the library and to restrain them from entering the class on Friday. Then in dramatic style I informed the class of a special noon rally to take place on Friday. This would be a rally for Third Wave members only.

It was a wild gamble. I just kept talking, afraid that if I stopped, someone would laugh or ask a question and the grand scheme would dissolve in chaos. I explained how at noon on Friday a national candidate for president would announce the formation of a Third Wave Youth Program. Simultaneous to this announcement more than a thousand youth groups from every part of the country would stand up and display their support for such a movement.

I confided that they were the students selected to represent our area. I also asked if they could make a good showing, because the press had been invited to record the event. No one laughed. There was not a murmur of resistance—quite the contrary, in fact. A fever pitch of excitement swelled across the room. "We can do it!" "Should we wear white shirts?" "Can we bring friends?" "Mr. Jones, have you seen this advertisement in *Time* magazine?"

The clincher came quite by accident. It was a full-page color advertisement in the current issue of *Time* for some lumber products. The advertiser identified his product as the Third Wave. The ad proclaimed in big red, white, and blue letters, "The Third Wave is coming." "Is this part of the campaign, Mr. Jones?" "Is it a code or something?"

"Yes. Now listen carefully. It's all set for tomorrow. Be in the small auditorium ten minutes before noon. Be seated. Be ready to display the discipline, community, and pride you have learned. Don't talk to anyone about this. This rally is for members only."

STRENGTH THROUGH UNDERSTANDING

On Friday, the final day of the exercise, I spent the early morning preparing the auditorium for the rally. At eleven-thirty students began to trickle into the room—at first a few, scouting the way, and then more. Row after row began to fill. A hushed silence shrouded the room. Third Wave banners hung like clouds over the assembly.

At twelve o'clock sharp I closed the room and placed guards at each door. Several friends of mine, posing as reporters and photographers, began to interact with the crowd, taking pictures and jotting frantic descriptive notes. A group photograph was taken. More than 200 students were crammed into the room. Not a vacant seat could be found. The group seemed to be composed of students from many persuasions. There were the athletes, the social prominents, the student leaders, the loners, the group of kids who always left school early, the bikers, the pseudo-hip, a few representatives of the school's dadaist clique, and some of the students who hung out at the laundromat. The entire collection, however, looked like one force as they sat in perfect attention. Every person was focusing on the TV set I had in the front of the room. No one moved. The room was empty of sound. It was like we were all witnesses to a birth. The tension and anticipation were beyond belief.

"Before turning on the national press conference, which begins in five minutes, I want to demonstrate to the press the extent of our training." With that, I gave the salute, which was followed automatically by 200 arms stabbing a reply. I then said the words "Strength through discipline," again followed by a repetitive chorus. We did this again and again. Each time the response was louder. The photographers were circling the ritual, snapping pictures, but by now they were ignored. I reiterated the importance of this event and asked once more for a show of allegiance. It was the last time I would ask anyone to recite. The room rocked with a guttural cry, "Strength through discipline."

It was 12:05. I turned off the lights in the room and walked quickly to the television set. The air in the room seemed to be drying up. It felt hard to breathe and even harder to talk. It was as if the climax of shouting souls had pushed everything out of the room. I switched the television set on. I was now standing next to the television, directly facing the room full of people. The machine came to life, producing a luminous field of phosphorous light.

Robert was at my side. I whispered to him to watch closely and pay attention to the next few minutes. The only light in the room was coming from the television, and it played against the faces in the room. Eyes strained and pulled at the light, but the pattern didn't change. The room stayed deadly still. Waiting. There was a mental tug-of-war between the people in the room and the television. The television won. The white glow of the test pattern didn't snap into the vision of a political candidate. It just whined on. Still the viewers persisted. There must be a program. It must be coming on. Where is it? The trance with the television continued for what seemed like hours. It was 12:07. Nothing. A blank field of white. It's not going to happen. Anticipation turned to anxiety and then to frustration. Someone stood up and shouted.

"There isn't any leader, is there?" Everyone turned in

shock, first to the despondent student and then back to the
television. Their faces held looks of disbelief.

In the confusion of the moment I moved slowly
toward the television. I turned if off. I felt air rush back into
the room. The room remained in fixed silence, but for the
first time I could sense people breathing. Students were
withdrawing their arms from behind their chairs. I expected a flood of questions but got intense silence. I began
to talk. Every word seemed to be taken and absorbed.

"Listen closely, I have something important to tell
you. Sit down. There is no leader! There is no such thing as
a national youth movement called the Third Wave. You
have been used. Manipulated. Shoved by your own desires
into the place you now find yourselves. You are no better or
worse than the German Nazis we have been studying. You
thought that you were the elect, that you were better than
those outside this room. You bargained your freedom for
the comfort of discipline and superiority. You chose to accept the group's will and the Big Lie over your own convic-
tions. Oh, you think to yourselves that you were just going
along for the fun, that you could have extricated yourselves
at any moment. But where were you heading? How far
would you have gone? Let me show you your future."

With that I switched on a rear-screen projector. It
quickly illuminated a white dropcloth hanging behind the
television. Large numbers appeared in a countdown. The
roar of the Nurenburg Rally blasted into vision. My heart
was pounding. In ghostly images the history of the Third
Reich paraded into the room. The discipline, the march of
super race. The Big Lie. Arrogance, violence, terror. People
being pushed into vans. The visual stench of death camps.
Faces without eyes. The trials. The plea of ignorance. I was
only doing my job. My job. As abruptly as it started, the

film froze to a halt on a single written frame: "Everyone must accept the blame—no one can claim that he didn't in some way take part."

The room stayed dark as the final footage of film flapped against the projector. I felt sick to my stomach. The room sweated and smelled like a locker room. No one moved. It was as if everyone wanted to dissect the moment, figure out what had happened. As if awakening from a dream and deep sleep, the entire room of people took one last look back into their consciousness. I waited for several minutes to let everyone catch up.

In the still-darkened room I began the explanation. I confessed my feeling of sickness and remorse. I told the assembly that a full explanation would take quite a while. But I'd start. I sensed myself moving from an introspective participant in the event toward the role of teacher. It's easier being a teacher. In objective terms I began to describe the past events.

"Through the experience of the past week we have all tasted what it was like to live and act in Nazi Germany. We learned what it felt like to create a disciplined social environment. To build a special society. Pledge allegiance to that society. Replace reason with rules. Yes, we would all have made good Germans. We would have put on the uniform. Turned our heads as friends and neighbors were cursed and then persecuted. Pulled the locks shut. Worked in the "defense" plants. Burned ideas. Yes, we know in a small way what it feels like to find a hero. To grab quick solutions. Feel strong and in control of destiny. We know the fear of being left out. The pleasure of doing something right and being rewarded. To be number one. To be right. Taken to an extreme, we have seen and perhaps felt what these actions will lead to. We have seen that fascism is not just something those other people did. No, it's right here. In this room. In our own personal habits and way of life. Scratch the surface and it appears. Something in all of us. We carry it like a disease. The belief that human beings are basically evil and therefore unable to act well toward each other. A belief that demands a strong leader and discipline to preserve social order. And there is something else. The act of apology.

"This is the final lesson to be experienced. This last lesson is perhaps the one of greatest importance. This lesson was the question that started our plunge into studying Nazi life. Do you remember the question? It concerned a bewilderment at the German populace claiming ignorance and noninvolvement in the Nazi movement. If I remember the question, it went something like this. How could the German soldier, teacher, railroad conductor, nurse, tax collector, the average citizen, claim at the end of the Third Reich that they knew nothing of what was going on? How can a people be a part of something and then claim at the demise that they were not really involved? What causes people to blank out their own history? In the next few minutes—and perhaps years—you will have an opportunity to answer this question.

"If our enactment of the fascist mentality is complete, not one of you will ever admit to being at this final Third Wave rally. Like the Germans, you will have trouble admitting to yourselves that you came this far. You will not allow your friends and parents to know that you were willing to give up individual freedom and power for the dictates of order and unseen leaders. You can't admit to being manipulated. Being a follower. To accepting the Third Wave as a way of life. You won't admit to participating in this madness. You will keep this day and this rally a secret. It's a secret I shall share with you."

I took the film from the three cameras in the room and pulled the celluloid into the exposing light. The deed was concluded. The trial was over. The Third Wave had ended.

I glanced over my shoulder. Robert was crying. Students slowly rose from their chairs and, without words, filed into the outdoor light. I walked over to Robert and threw my arms around him. Robert was sobbing—taking in large uncontrollable gulps of air, and saying, "It's over."

"It's all right." In our consoling each other we became a rock in the stream of exiting students. Some swirled back to momentarily hold Robert and me. Others cried openly and then brushed away tears to carry on. Human beings circling and holding each other. Moving toward the door and the world outside.

For a week in the middle of a school year we had shared fully in life. And as predicted, we also shared a deep secret. In the four years I taught at Cubberley High School no one ever admitted to attending the Third Wave rally. Oh, we talked and studied our actions intently. But the rally itself—no. It was something we all wanted to forget.

The Acorn People

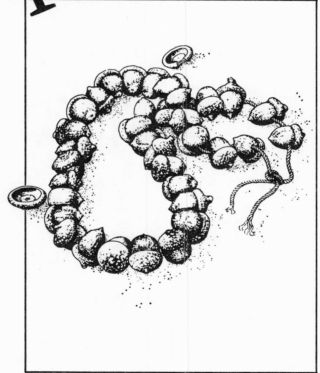

Day 1

Children spilled from cars and buses. It was an eerie sight. Parents carefully picked children from their perches and placed them in wheelchairs. There was an open-mouthed silence. The woods and paths of Camp Wiggin were accustomed to troops of running feet and the noise of children at play. With these wheelchair children there was only silence. It was as if the woods themselves were watching the unfolding of chairs and the lifting of bodies. All life seemed to stop. In procession, the parents wheeled their children toward awaiting counselors. I was a counselor. A target of this pilgrimage. Like everyone around me, I didn't know what to say.

Oh shit. What do you say to a parade of children who move toward you only by the energy of their parents' insistence? Who move toward you with swollen heads of gargantuan proportion. With birth scars that have left the eyes without sight or the body without arms and legs. Children who seem drained of expression. Pulled into convulsions by unseen strings. Pallid in color and spirit. Beings without visible life. Crumpled and stuffed into wheelchairs. Covered with blankets, to ward off not the cold, but the vision of disfigurement.

The camp nurse had given us a one-day orientation about handicapped children, but to see this mass of injury stunned the brain. There were perhaps one hundred twenty children in all. They seemed old for their age. I remember the nurse saying, "Most will not live past their teen years. It is nature's way." She described the hydrocephalic children with heads that looked like melons about to burst. And the disease of multiple sclerosis, which ate away at the muscles, leaving the body without energy or movement. The children who had mongoloid faces and a distant stare. Children with an epileptic chemistry, which at any moment could jerk the body into an unconscious spasm. Children living with an unexplained polio attack that would cruelly freeze their legs in place, leaving the rest of the body and mind to wonder at the reason for this paralysis. And finally the children who entered life without vision or a hand or perhaps a face.

The transfer of children from parent to camp staff was like a precious stamp being traded by collectors. No sign of real welcome or excitement. The stamp had value but no voice. It was one more exchange. Parents, weary of the drive and the emotion of parting, didn't say much. They paused, mentioned how nice the camp looked, and said goodbye.

Counselors welcomed their new responsibilities with an equal degree of decorum. There were two counselors for each cabin of five children. I shared counseling duties with Dominic Cavelli from New York. He was a tall Italian youth with a slight but strong body, deep brown eyes that told you of his concern and love for children, and a soft manner and smile that moved across his face whenever he was about to speak. He was after a career working with handicapped children, whereas I had placed myself in this position merely for the job. Oh, I rationalized about serving others and compassion for kids, but behind this mask was a simple wish to have a good-paying job for a few weeks and to enjoy summer camp life. I had been a P.E. student and athlete in college. The thought of playing with kids, swimming all day, and taking long hikes had drawn me to this place. My illusions were quickly clouded and washed away. I wasn't about to frolic with these children. We would be lucky, I thought, if we could even take a few steps together.

As the children were assembled for cabin assignments, I wondered at this mass of humanity before me. These children with hollowed-out faces and nervous twitches. What were they thinking? Did they think? Or even feel? They all looked alike. Boys and girls inseparable by a common hurt. Did they have hopes for the future? Or was life a dulling repetition of survival? Or worse, some kind of perverted game?

I didn't have time to think. There was work to do. Every movement required a tug and a pull. Just crossing the camp from assembly point to cabin took twenty minutes per child. Some could be pushed; others had to be carried or patiently guided. Dominic and I, like the other counselors, swept back and forth freighting luggage, children, and the "ditty bag" that would inevitably spill to the ground.

We didn't have any experience at this task, and the camp wasn't set up for this kind of care. Each cabin had three steps. Steps that became hurdles. You can't wheel a chair straight up a set of stairs. I tried that with one kid and spilled him head first. Everything had to be learned. The simplest task was an ordeal.

The camp was divided into two rows of cabins. Boys on one side, girls on the other. At one end of the rows stood the camp bathroom, dining hall, swimming pool, and flagpole. The flagpole had a large speaker on it that barked a greeting to all campers and played songs left over from the Boy Scouts who normally inhabited the camp. In the midst of this orchestrated hello, I was silently cursing toilets that didn't have grab bars. No sooner had one kid gotten unpacked and comfortable than it was off to the bathroom. What had always been a simple and normal act became a trial. Pants had to be pulled over cumbersome braces that grabbed and pinched at anything within reach. I had never changed someone's pants, much less balanced a child on the toilet, only to be told in crying sobs that "I don't have to go now!" Back with the pants. Lifting and tugging until at last I realize I'm sitting in the wheelchair and a wet child is now sitting in my lap. (It would be humorous once, but this struggle becomes routine.) It covers every minute and every thought, grating and shredding away any pretense or possibility for even the simplest of interaction. Every move, be it brushing teeth or simply rolling over, requires assistance. I feel like a slave and resent it.

The first evening meal was something I looked forward to. At last, the chance to sit down and eat. Dominic and I got our kids down to the hall by moving in shifts. At the table the loudspeaker once again reminded us we were on foreign turf. There was a Boy Scout prayer and then food. I started eating. Then realized that half the kids couldn't feed themselves. With unshielded anger, I started pumping spoonfuls of peas and potatoes into open mouths. Any semblance of good will or sympathy was gone. My liberal do-goodism lasted one afternoon and I wanted out.

By evening I was exhausted and angry. I questioned the camp, the loudspeaker that kept us moving, and myself. I couldn't get close to the kids and didn't want to. A fear emerged in my mind that this illness surrounding me would

somehow rub off. That if I touched a disfigured limb or
body, I could be poisoning myself. In a nightmare I dreamed
of children's legs and heads unscrewing. Parts of bodies
coming off in my hands.

DAY 2

Morning greeted our cabin not with the warmth of
the sun, but with a chilling cold and the smell of urine.
Three kids had wet their beds through. A fourth had rolled
over on a urine bag, causing it to burst. In a stupor Dominic
and I began the cleanup and morning runs to the bathroom.
The loudspeaker hurried everyone to breakfast with a
trumpet: "You gotta get up, you gotta get up . . ." What a
joke!

It was noisy at breakfast. For the first time, I felt the
kids' presence as individuals. Each of them watching Dominic and me. Stealing a glimpse and then staring. Perhaps
looking at us for the first time. Seeing if we would stay. It
wasn't a challenge but a real question. I felt it. I looked
back.

The first of our kids was Benny B. Benny was black,
peanut in size. Polio had taken his legs but not his gall or
heart. He was the most mobile kid at camp. One kid that
Dominic and I didn't have to push or help with the toilet.
He was his own man. Most kids have a "thing" they do.
Something special. For Benny B. it was speed. With a crash
helmet pulled tightly over his head, he hunched forward in
his wheelchair like a dirt-track driver in a stock car. Once
snuggly into position he reared back with both arms, giving
the chair a rocking motion that could be thrust forward at
incredible speed. He peeled rubber and was off. Hydroplaning across the dusty floor. Then spinning and heading
back to the cabin. Finishing the dash with a "wheelie" that

only he could do. The spokes on Benny's chair were decorated with stickers and reflectors. At night he was a light streaker through camp. On the back webbing of his chair was the name of this speed freak, Benny B.

Spider was another kid in our cabin. It was a funny name because Spider didn't have any legs or arms. He had stumps that stuck out from his short frame like broken branches out of a tree. Like Benny, Spider was alert and perceptive. You could tell by his eyes. Children handicapped by illness that floods the brain with fluid or strikes off oxygen at birth seem to stare without seeing. Attention seems pulled by a constantly moving magnet. Eyes seem cloudy—unable to sparkle or hold on to anything. Spider's eyes held everything. And what his eyes couldn't hold, his mouth tried to trap. Spider loved to talk and talk and talk. It was like being in the presence of a juke box. The only difference was that this machine was self-operative. Spider had to be fed, but even that didn't stop him. He just talked, swallowed, and talked some more.

Far less active and alert than Benny B. or Spider was Thomas Stewart. He had multiple sclerosis, the cruelest ailment of all. Thomas must have been fifteen or maybe sixteen. It was hard to tell. Benny B. and Spider looked and acted like the eight- and ten-year-olds they were. But Thomas—it was hard to know anything about him. All the children were light in weight but Thomas was the lightest. He weighed about 35 pounds. Picking him up was like holding a collapsible tent. He just gave way. There was no center of gravity. His bones seemed unconnected. Indeed, that's what the disease had done. Over eleven years it had slowly and certainly robbed Thomas of the fiber and muscle that held his body together. (I think the act of watching and feeling this gave Thomas an awareness of the deteriora-

tion of his own body not felt by children afflicted from birth.) Thomas had eyes that seemed like wells. They locked up secrets. His mouth was always dry—almost crusted over. Pinched tight, as if to hold out the invading air or hold in some final scream. He watched the world about him but gave nothing to it. He was sullen, hunched over in his chair, always covered by a dark blanket. Unwilling to move unless moved. Pensive, patient, and dying.

Martin was the most able-bodied child in our group. Like other blind children in camp he had a constant smile and seemed in perpetual motion. Sitting still, he would rock forward and back. Even standing, he swayed rhythmically. I wondered what sound or unseen tide pulled at him. Martin was extremely likable and outgoing. He was about fourteen, tall and slender, with bright red hair that stuck out in every direction. In strident steps he would march across the camp grounds. I was amazed at how straight he always walked. In many ways he seemed to navigate like a ship. He could sense tree limbs and moving objects at head level. His only sensory block seemed to be at ground level. A slight indentation or tree root would cause a faltering followed by a stream of cussing. It was self-cursing; not directed at the obstacle, but at himself for not "seeing" it. Martin seemed a good kid. A little older and wiser than Benny B. or Spider and more demanding of himself than Thomas Stewart or Arid.

Arid was the fifth kid under our charge. He got his nickname from his smell. It was awful. Arid or Aaron Gerwalski didn't have a bladder or the normal means to pull waste from the body. His skin was always clammy. A large water-bottle-looking bag was attached to his intestines. The bag, strapped to his leg, collected a urine waste that had to be emptied every hour. He hated his own smell as much as those around him hated it. Arid wasn't a humorous name. This condition was terrible for anyone to carry, but for a young teenager it must have been overwhelming. The smell repelled any gesture of friendship. It stalled and interrupted any conversation before it could begin.

There you have it. The kids were gutsy and maybe even the basis for lots of self-awareness, but I wasn't enamored by the prospect. I mean this wasn't the way the job description read. Maybe I could deal with one child, but the thought of responding to such a thunder of pain, well, I couldn't do it. I wanted to go home. To get to the beach. To run as fast as I could. Lie in the warm sun. Breathe in deep gulps of ocean air. Anything but care for this carnage. I couldn't do it. And I didn't want to try and fake it.

In our first day of activity we were assigned to the craft area in the morning and swimming in the afternoon. I contemplated getting sick or being called away to a family emergency. I also realized that I was afraid of any action. I was afraid to leave and face the thought that "I couldn't take it." And I was afraid to stay for the same reason. There was no bravery or conviction in my action. I simply decided to stay. Like Thomas Stewart, I would close off all thoughts. I would endure.

At the craft table I rounded up Benny B., got Martin to work with Spider, and gave the quiet Thomas Stewart and Arid each a private work space. Dominic went to scout the pool area and determine what kind of water activities we might get into. The craft table was full of leftover Boy Scout materials and sample projects. There were whistles, hatchet holsters, Indian headdresses, and bookends made out of pine cones. I busied myself with a nut necklace. It was an act of frustration. At least it symbolized how I felt. Crazy to be here. Absolutely crazy.

Benny B. asked what I was making and I told him, "A necklace." He could see it wasn't a designated project. Spider asked what the necklace was for. And asked. And asked. Finally I blurted, "I feel a little weird being here, so I've made myself a necklace of nuts." Spider didn't stop or recoil; he just laughed, "So do we, counselor, we're all a little nutty here!" Benny added, "You might call us the nut people, yeah, that's a good name for us." I turned to Spider to tell him, "My name isn't counselor, it's Ron." He was already off with another question, "Mr. Counselor, Ron, can we make a necklace like yours?" "Sure, I said."

When Dominic returned we had a surprise for him. His very own acorn necklace. Benny B. had raced about collecting every nut in sight. Spider told him where most of them could be found. Martin strung most of them together. Arid was delighted by the smell. Thomas Stewart by the gift. Within this brief encounter we all had this crazy necklace in common.

As we moved toward the pool, the other kids noticed our necklaces. Spider was quick to explain the sight. "We're the Acorn People. Can't you see?" So we were dubbed and christened by our own act. Like it or not, we became the Acorn People. My fellow travelers and I were now drawn together like blood brothers. We would share a common history and fate. We would endure together.

I'm glad I stayed. The swimming pool was a new world for everyone. The water gave bouyancy and freedom to our bodies and to the pent-up children in all of us. Each child was given an orange safety belt and carefully lifted into the pool. That's where the careful and restricted movement ended and the teasing, splashing, racing began. Children and counselors held in bondage to chairs and harnesses were free. It was as if the water gave us permission to push each other and not just be pushed. We were comic aliens on a strange liquid planet. Popping up and down in the water, we held each other and bobbed in unison to create huge waves. Chased about like orange speedboats. Squirted and spit at each other. Or just relaxed and let the current of play move us about. Imagined sharks and sea monsters, and pincher bugs. Yelled and screamed.

Each kid approached the water in a delightful way. Arid had to paddle about in an inner tube, holding his bag above the water. It was his secret weapon. He threatened to squirt anyone who splashed him. It was an effective threat. Benny B. grabbed a tube and—you guessed it—he became the pool's fastest inner tube. Arms flailing away like a windmill, he looked like a pool-cleaning machine gone berserk. If Benny was the speed king of the pool, Thomas Stewart was the luxury cruise ship. In elegant grace Thomas ended up sitting on three inner tubes, quietly riding the waves made by the rest of us. As for Martin, he was the classic submarine. The pressure of the water and the resonant noise of the pool seemed to give Martin a keen sense of what was happening. I watched him dodge and chase Benny B. with radar intensity. His greatest pleasure, however, was a real fright. For some reason he simply loved to unlock his belt and sink to the bottom of the pool. He would sit there crosslegged and motionless until his lungs called for breath or I reached down and grabbed him by his red hair. Thank God for that red hair. It was like a buoy that signaled for lifting. Of all the children in camp, Spider was the most amazing phenomenon in water. Just as I was about to commit myself to holding him in the pool he said he wanted to show me something. Spider could swim. I propped him up at the edge of the pool as he instructed and then waited in the water to catch him. With a head-first plunge he was in the water and pulling himself through it like a dolphin. His body seemed to lengthen out and undulate. First the head would surface, take a breath, then shoot downward, only to arc back to the surface and dive again. With this repeated whip-like motion Spider could swim. In watching Spider move with the water and use its turbulence I thought of the fear he must have faced the first time in water and the endurance that allowed him to come to terms with this fear.

As our session in the pool ended Spider put on a demonstration of his ability by swimming the length of the pool. Several groups of children from other cabins gathered about, all watching intently this single figure submerge and surface its way across the pool. I don't think Spider had ever swum this distance. His movement in the water had slowed and almost stopped when he finally nudged the end of the pool. When I lifted him from the water his entire face broke into a grin. There were whoops and smiles from everyone. It was not a smile I was familiar with. Not the smile of a raucous ego or aggressive threat, but the smile of knowing. The blind children show this emotion best of all. It's as if their whole face lights up. Everyone was smiling with Spider. Me too.

In our second evening of camp the Acorn Society had its first meeting. The camp loudspeaker had blared its goodnight. A lantern was our only light. It was a warm light that matched my feelings. Everyone was accounted for. Heads cranked out of sleeping bags to meet the flickering shadows. To stay in touch. A long day had passed. But we made it. I sensed that the trial was shared. It was hard on everyone. I retreated in thought, remembering how Benny had cried in the bathroom when I tried to change him. I was mad at the time; he must have been hurt and humiliated at the rough treatment I gave him. The day was full of a minutiae of events. Small victories. Just getting by was super. I felt good. I could make it. There were events like the acorn necklaces and Spider's swim to keep us all going. Dominic broke into this silent thinking. We all were just looking at each other. Dominic called the meeting to order and then proceeded to tell Mafia stories. His breath danced into the cold air. I fell asleep with Mafia gangsters and gun molls running around in my mind chasing a group of kids wearing acorns around their necks.

DAY 3

That goddamned camp loudspeaker should be shot. It's warm and cozy and I don't want to get up. The floor is cold and the wheelchairs and leg braces chill the touch. Like a cavalry unit Cabin Four is getting harnessed for the day. I disconnect Aaron's bladder bag and run down to the bathroom to dump it. It's at least warm. No one has wet a bed. Yippee! I'm amazed at how quickly Dominic and I have adapted to the task of getting everyone dressed and moving. The cabin is very confining. Definitely not built for wheelchairs. For the first time I sense it and it's spoken about. We are all beginning to look forward to the day ahead. In our morning trudge to breakfast I noticed I still had on my acorn necklace. Dominic observed my discovery and pointed that he did also. So did Benny and Thomas. We all did. The Acorn People were on the move.

Camp Wiggin was administered by a retired army colonel, Mr. Bradshaw. He had a ruddy complexion and a manner that matched. He administered the camp like a mandarin war lord. One day he would be at breakfast reading orders and "thoughts for the camper" and the next day he would be gone. The following day he would swoop into camp with visiting dignitaries, give another set of directives, and be off again. What he left in his wake was a set of regulations and schedules that were hand-me-downs from the scouts. They might have made sense to a group of troopers who could move between the craft center and the pool in five minutes. For us, each move was a campaign. Just getting to the pool took half an hour, with another half hour to get out of clothing and ready for the water. The recreational schedule of the camp was laid out in hourly blocks. It went something like this: Breakfast, 8:00; Crafts, 9:00; Hiking, 10:00; Study in the meadow, 11:00; Lunch, 12:00; Open recreation, 1:00; Swimming, 2:00; Dinner, 4:00; Campfire, 6:00; Taps, 7:30. It was a masterful plan, for scoutmasters. For us, it was out of the question. Each group of three cabins would rotate about the camp on its own schedule. It was like a merry-go-round. We were always moving, getting ready to move, or finishing a move. Out of the corner of our eyes we could see everyone else engaged in a similar pursuit. Besides the obvious problem of never having enough time to really do anything, this carousel schedule kept the kids from meeting other kids. You were always with the same group. This meant boys and girls were never together. Oh. Perhaps that was the reason behind all this. Dominic and I decided at breakfast to talk with the kids about the day ahead as if we could plan it ourselves. Following breakfast we would go directly to the pool. The decision was unanimous.

The pool was being used by a group of girls. I could see the headlines: "Group of boys wearing nothing but acorn necklaces attacks girls in the camp pool!" That's not quite the way it happened. Participants in this first-ever "integrated swim" were self-conscious and then flirtatious in a typically pubescent way. The boys worried about their trunks being tightly tied. And their hair. My God, I had to comb their hair before they would venture out to poolside. The boys kept to one side of the pool. The girls attached themselves to the other like a string of pearls. Soon, like melting ice cream, the sun and water worked their magic. Children—no, young adults, no, children—were playing the games of dunk and run or just plain show-off. With coy glances and gossipy chatter the girls attracted the boys' attention. Even Thomas Stewart, the most distant of all, putted about the pool in his barge of tubes and orange jackets. I caught him smiling for the first time when he oh so slightly nudged a girl in an equally high pile of tubes. They were playing bumper cars in a soft but deliberate way. It was almost erotic. Bumping and touching each other through the elasticity and movement of the tubes.

All my questions about sex and the handicapped were answered in front of my gaze. If ever there was a dance of affection, with taunts and prowess and just plain sexual play, it was taking place in the splashes and noise before me. Our red-haired submarine found three girls of similar inclination and down they went. Arid was being pushed by Benny B. and a group of younger girls. They eventually made a chain of bobbing bodies that moved around and around the pool, interrupted by occasional water fights and screams of enjoyment. By the end of the hour, kids were helping and teaching each other their unique water tricks. There was a great deal of speculation as to who had a crush on whom. Spider had it all figured out. He had a mate for everyone at camp. As for himself, well, it was a toss-up between two of the women counselors. He liked older women.

Dressing took place at record speed. There was a new excitement in the air. Leaving the pool area with a cluster of children, I noticed that a blind girl named Mary was wearing an acorn necklace. She was a tall angular girl with a kind face and a warm smile. She seemed to be aware of our presence as we started up the hill toward our cabin. I turned to Martin. He still had on his necklace. So did Thomas. The question of how she got the necklace slid from my mind and then back again with a rush as Arid complained, "I've lost my necklace . . . hey, can we stop so I can make another?" There was a chuckle at this revelation. Benny asked, "Where did you lose it?" Spider and Benny B. chided together, "Couldn't be you gave it to Mary . . . could it?" Arid looked slightly sick and then relieved as Martin saved the day with an idea. "Let's make a bunch of necklaces, OK?" Benny, not letting go, "Yeah, we can give them to our girlfriends." Thomas Stewart surprised us all by talking. He just didn't say much. His words were brief. "Not a bad idea."

We set about making acorn necklaces by the gross. By the end of the afternoon we had successfully cornered the acorn necklace market. There wasn't an acorn anywhere in sight. Not one. Benny wore his necklaces and he stuffed into suitcases those he couldn't wear. The others simply hung the treasure from their chairs. Throughout the days that followed they gave them to everyone. The entire camp—kids, counselors, cooks, and even Mrs. Nelson, the old nurse—became Acorn Society members.

DAY 6

The breakup of the schedule and the giving of the necklaces drew the camp together and gave us all a feeling of confidence and a penchant for adventure. One particular adventure, I shall never forget. It was the mountain. Our interest and knowledge of the hill came from the everpresent loudspeaker. One evening the normal recorded taps and Boy Scout pledge were followed by an announcement that special merit badges would be awarded to all those completing the climb to Lookout Mountain.

Benny B. picked up this errant message. "If the Boy Scouts can climb that mountain, can we?" Dominic and I exchanged glances of doubt and surprise. Our thoughts were picked up. Spider sided with Benny. Thomas was quiet. Arid didn't think it was too neat an idea. Martin just stood there, and then with all our attention fixed on him he started stamping his feet in an exaggerated march step. Hefting his knee high and then softly pulling his foot to the floor. Then with his whole body in movement he pumped his arms and in mime fashion demonstrated that he was going to climb that mountain. He was marching off to Pretoria. There was nothing to do but follow.

In the morning we made plans to find and climb Lookout Mountain. Maps in the camp office gave the trail markings and location of the mountain. It was a six-mile hike round trip. We had no idea of the terrain. For supplies we took a bag of apples, some carrots, raisins, canteens of water, and three kitchen knives. The knives were for protection. Like a military convoy we broke from camp at the first sign of morning. As we passed down the rows of cabins a few sleepy campers heard our clanking progress and asked where we were going. Benny was our voice, "To Lookout Mountain."

Dominic led the way pushing Spider. Next came Benny B. wheeling himself, followed by Martin pushing Arid. I took up the rear of the column pushing Thomas Stewart. We looked and sounded like a wagon train. Like the pioneers before us, our faces were pushed into silence by the unknown that lay ahead. There was little talk and a strange absence of humor. A sense of fear overwhelmed any thought of adventure. Each curve in the trail presented an obstacle.

Our greatest hardship was trailside bushes and branches. They slashed against the wheels and, if we were not careful, entwined themselves like tentacles around the spokes and footrests. Forging through this undergrowth reminded me of Humphrey Bogart's voyage of the *African Queen*. The trail kept getting narrower. It went from a walkway to a path to a skinny trail. As the trail narrowed, our effort to push the chairs increased tremendously. In methodic lunges we crossed fields and cut into a dark wood. For the first time in my experience of pushing a wheelchair I felt Thomas shift and lift his weight in an effort to ease the strain of movement. It was a slight adjustment but it meant he was pulling his body as hard as I was pushing. I strained ahead to see that Arid and Spider were equally at work, lifting their weight and pushing branches aside, using whatever energy they had to help our progress. The trail started upward. We had to turn around and pull the chairs from behind. Benny was forced to pull his wheels and then brake with each stroke. Our movement was reduced to pull, stop. Pull, stop. Pull.

Perspiring and heaving for breath, I was haunted by the thought of going back. I just didn't want to turn around. It would be better to inch our way forever than to stop. Pull. Stop. Within this exertion my thoughts wandered. I felt the sensation of escape experienced in long-distance running. It's as if the mind detaches from the body. In flight it finds refreshment in abstract wonder. I pondered the condition in which people work at intricate tasks and behavior without knowing where they are headed. Surely that is the situation I am in. Where am I going? And why am I at the base of this mountain fighting to see the top? Is it the climb that's important? Or the summit? Can it be both? Or something else? Perhaps it's how we go down from the hill that counts. Or is it in simply enduring that we find the strength and purpose we seek?

Reaching exhaustion, Benny had to stop. He didn't say a word. Just stopped pushing. His chair slowly slid to a halt against Martin. Like a train being derailed we twisted to a halt. Chairs and bodies stacked upon each other. Without giving anyone the chance to think about our predicament Spider started talking. In a shrill and quick voice he began playing the role of expedition padre. Dramatically taking his canteen he sprinkled water on the hillside and proclaimed, "I hereby name this place Benny's Landing." Everyone looked up. Spider was still talking, "And claim this place and all its riches for The Acorn Society." He crossed himself and blessed the soil. Finding a willing audience Spider continued, "Mr. Thomas, I appoint you expedition recorder. Martin, you're expeditionary leader. You counselors, you're, let's see, you're soldiers. Benny, you're our scout." The drama gave us a chance to relax and realize our accomplishment. To look around for the first time in our journey. Feel the warmth of the day and the aroma of damp grass. We were in the rib of a small hill. The sun angled through the trees as if in search of someone. It splintered against the mass of rising moisture and cascaded to the ground. The air was heavy, full of light and flying things. We seemed surrounded by a soft but definable noise. A humming of insects on the move. Leaves turning to the sun. Seeds in flight. Morning dew evaporating and billowing upward. The ground drying and pulling tight.

Everyone seemed entranced by our discovery. Here we were sitting in the middle of a forest with wheelchairs, an experience that had only known city streets and "convenience ramps." Spider again broke the concentration. "Well," he said, "what are you waiting for, Aaron? You're the expedition cook; break out the food." Spider was still talking as we took up the food, passed it around, and started eating. "We have more places to explore than this place, you know." With this moment of rest and Spider's encouragement our journey became enjoyable. We knew there were more places to meet, and with some patience we would find them. And so we started off again. Benny, pleased to have a place named after him, was thrilled that each time we halted there would be a similar honor. Sure enough, we "discovered" and marked our progress with Benny's Rock, Benny's Fall, Benny's Number 2 (in reference to a toilet break), and Benny's Vista . . . .

By the end of the morning we had climbed steadily into the foothills toward Lookout Mountain. Spider was talking all the way. Naming birds, plants, and historic sights of interest. Thomas was keeping a mental diary, repeating points of importance to Benny and the rest of us. Arid was directing our culinary use of supplies and dreaming up delicious ice cream sodas and banana splits. Martin seemed to spread out. He swung erratically from side to side in his effort to pull Aaron. His head moved constantly as if it were an antenna tracking some wondrous delight. Spider finally ran out of things to name or count. Without hesitation he created and performed what he called the "Acorn Marching Song." If you've ever heard the slave song "Mary Mac," you will have some notion of the noise we made crossing the wilderness.

After our succession of ceremonious starts and stops we reached the final grade to the summit. We had covered over two-and-a-half miles. The final half mile looked straight up. More forbidding than the incline, however, was the deterioration of the trail. It simply stopped. The final grade was a hillside of slate rock and loose gravel.

There would be no way to pull or push the chairs up this. The wheels simply spun around for lack of traction. Spider called this place "Desperation," but no one laughed. Dominic suggested, "How about us trying to carry everyone?" Thomas nixed the idea, "Not me, I'm not going up there on someone's back." Aaron had a similar plan, "I'll watch." Spider and Benny were talking wildly about a movie they saw in which climbers used ropes and things. During our deliberation Martin had moved several feet up the hill without our noticing. He called down to us, "Hey you guys, it's easy." Martin was sitting down, facing downhill. By moving his legs under him in a squat position and then pushing back, he edged up the hill in this sitting posture. He looked like he was rowing a boat. Only instead of rowing across water he was literally rowing up the hill on his bottom. Using legs and arms in an accordion fashion he made steady progress. Benny was delighted, "Martin, you're amazing." Spider added to the compliment, "Make sure that man gets the mountain cross." Thomas and Aaron were still doubtful. Leaving their wheelchairs was not an easy thing to do.

After a long debate and several demonstrations by Martin, we decided to make the ascent. Dominic sat against the hill and I placed Spider in his lap. Using belt buckles and safety straps from the wheelchairs I tied the two together. Dominic tried a few rows up the hill. It worked. Spider strapped to Dominic's stomach gave both of them the opportunity to look down the hill as they inched upward. It also freed Dominic's legs and arms for the hinge-like movement and balance necessary to squeeze up the hill and not slip back. Benny was next in line. He wanted to try it by himself. In a trial effort he worked his way up the hill and right out of his pants. With his insistence we tied a pillow from one of the chairs to his butt. He was ready. With his strength he just might be able to drag his body the distance. Martin and Aaron were next. Martin's confidence helped Aaron. In a sitting position Martin shaped his body and legs into a lap. I gently placed Aaron against Martin and bound them together. Thomas and I were at the end of the ladder. I sat on the ground in front of Thomas and pulled him first out of the chair and onto me. We twisted and rotated until both of us were comfortable. Then tied ourselves together.

Like a caterpillar we edged our way up the slate. The loose rock gave and slipped into pockets that could be used as footholds. Our trail looked like a smooth slide bordered by tractor-like gouges. I thought to myself how a hiker someday would discover our tracks and the Santa Cruz Mountains would have evidence of its very own Big Foot. Martin's invention was marvelous. Who would have thought of going uphill backwards, sitting on our bottoms? We moved in a syncopated rhythm. First the legs pushing against the hill, followed quickly by a push with both hands. We would stop to rest and then continue. (Observing the valley floor below us, we saw the tree line slipping beneath our vision, aware that we could now see valleys moving away from our vantage point like huge green waves.) At two o'clock, according to Spider, we reached the top of Lookout Mountain. He gently gave the mountain one of his necklaces. Not the act of a conqueror, but a friend. We had done it.

Like all accomplishments our attention shifted from the joy of lying across the peak of this mountain to another vision. The sky above us. Even Martin seemed to study the traces of clouds and the blueness of the space above us. It was strange, there was no jubilation. What had been the ultimate victory was now matter of fact. The sky beckoned our attention. It gave us peace. There were seven of us lying faces to the sky, just watching. A lonely piston-engine plane droned by. I love that distant whining sound. We grabbed for a mountain and found the sky. I don't think any of us had ever seen the sky in quite this way. The wheelchair and city life we all knew just didn't give us the chance to face the sky. It was wonderful. This must be the exhilaration that drives explorers. The surprise of always finding another vista, a new thought, an unexpected strength. The comrade-ship of doing something together. Doing something no one else would dare. And in the end finding something as simple and everpresent as the sky.

The return trip to camp seemed half the time. We passed things we knew and places that were familiar. We knew where we were going. It was a quiet return. Our pace increased as we approached camp. Perhaps it was the idea of a waiting dinner or the chance to tell everyone about our climb. We wouldn't tell about the sky. It was our secret.

We arrived late to the dining hall. In dusty halos we tramped and rolled in. I guess all explorers expect a ticker-tape parade of some kind. Surely the world knew of our ex-ploits. But the dining room was unexplainably quiet. Thoughts tumbled into the void. Did we do something wrong? Would Mr. Bradshaw drum us out of camp? Had something happened to one of the kids? What's going on? Where is the laughter, the questioning, the noise? It's as if we had left a party of friends and returned to find another set of people engaged in a ritual we knew nothing about. We blended into the silence rather that interrupt it. Became a part of the stillness. Ate quickly without much emotion, anxious to get outside and learn what was wrong. It was like the first day of camp. I felt afraid.

It didn't take long to find out what had happened.

The camp director, Mr. Bradshaw, had been "alarmed at the randomness of camp activities" and "concerned that parents visiting the camp on the following day would not find camp as it should be." To prepare the camp for Parent Visitation Day he announced strict adherence to the camp schedule. He had finished his remarks with ". . . We don't want to demonstrate *unruly behavior* at camp in front of our parents, now do we?"

We all knew what unruly behavior meant. Dominic had started teaching boys and girls the skills of cooking. He made up delicious meals. In fact, he was famous for his chopped hamburger, apple, cheese, and onion delight. It was a mixture of these ingredients rolled into a ball and covered with aluminum foil for cooking in an open fire. It was delicious but rather unruly. Especially since most of the food was swiped from the camp kitchen. Dominic began holding a late afternoon "eating club" attended regularly by forty or fifty kids. Aaron became assistant chef and apprentice. Most of these kids had never held a knife, let alone sliced a carrot. Dominic was a master at closing his eyes and trusting that determination could beat any palsy or lack of sight. He was right. Dominic's success with kids prompted other forms of unruly behavior.

Several women counselors had gotten interested in archery. They went to town and bought a set of inexpensive bows and arrows. It wasn't the safest place to be when they held their practice, but it was a thrill to watch children struggle to use their chairs and bodies as the means to hold the bow and draw an arrow. It was pure joy to watch arrows take flight following long moments of intensive effort and patience.

Another type of unruly conduct came from Lenny X. Lenny was a black African. He was mean looking. His face scarred and twisted. You wouldn't dare meet him if it were not for his songs. Wherever he went he would be humming or whistling. You couldn't help but join in. Pretty soon you'd be humming the same song, catch Lenny's eye and smile. One day Lenny X. sat down in a shady place and just started singing. It was just after lunch when he started. He sat in that one place and sang until late afternoon. By the time he finished, every child and counselor had learned Lenny's songs. It was such a relief from the Boy Scout anthems and bugle calls that pounced from the camp loudspeaker. Lenny taught songs that, once started, could go on forever. Evenings at camp were blessed by these sounds. One cabin would start and others would softly join in until everyone was singing. These were the most tranquil hours I have ever experienced. Lenny considered songs a greeting. He explained to the children that in America you greet someone with "How are you?", whereas in Europe the greeting is "Good day," and in China it's "Have you eaten?" "The greetings of Senegal and Gambia," Lenny explained, "are like their songs—they ask 'Do you have peace?'" His songs were like this greeting. They were expressions of peace.

The most unruly act of camp was perpetrated by the camp nurse, Mrs. Nelson. She was an older matronly looking woman who had probably served as a nurse in World War II. She always wore the same dark blue dress with matching socks rolled under at the ankles. The aging process had not been kind to Mrs. Nelson. Although she walked with a quick gait that bespoke a once-spry woman, she was now quite heavy. Her face was always over-made-up with bright red lipstick and swooping eyebrows. Well, it was just this sight that caught some of the girls' attention. They started asking to see how she did it. I guess this might have been the first time in a long while that anyone noticed this labored beauty. She responded by giving impromptu lessons in makeup for the girls. For most, this must have been their first taste of rouge. All of a sudden half the girls had bright red lipstick. The next day they smelled like a field of lilacs and all showed up wearing face cream. Of course they thought they were beautiful. Mr. Bradshaw saw them as unruly.

The prospect of ending Dominic's eating club, the straight-arrow archery team, Lenny's songfest, or Mrs. Nelson's beauty salon was out of the question. The children were learning, growing, and most important of all, they were happy. (I gauged my own change in these days by realizing what a benefit it was to be in this Boy Scout camp.) I walked around thanking stairs, bunk beds, and hills, because they made all of us behave a little more normally. The camp was not a place for handicapped children and the kids knew it. Camp Wiggin was a summer camp for children who could shoot arrows, cook goulash, take hikes, and sing songs. It wasn't a place for ramps, sanitized medical facilities, swimming pool rails, or activity schedules. It was a place for children and their expectations and fantasies for life.

DAY 7

The next morning was filled with orders. Each cabin had an assigned location. We were to display for the parents "what we do at camp." There were no protests or shouts of outrage. There were parents on the way. And you know. It was easier to follow directions. Our assignment was the craft area. Out came the headdress and bookends. According to Mr. Bradshaw, we were to make nametags. Using up a box of index cards we completed name plates for every child in camp. Dominic, Spider, and Martin went around delivering the tags. There were six boxes of blank cards still unused and plenty of time. Aaron was the first to see this and start to work. He scrawled a label for the Indian headdress. He carefully printed Indian Headdress and placed the card next to the artifact. Then he started on the bookends. Benny, Thomas, and I caught on. Each started marking tags for trees, wheelchairs, drinking fountain, pool, nurse's station, leaf, rock, cabin door, toilet door, table, handicapped child. Dominic and his messengers started acting like Santa Claus delivering the tags. Placing them on everything. Within an hour every moving and stationary item had a label. Some had two. The camp looked like it was hit by a bumper-sticker blizzard. In the middle of the paper storm the parents started to arrive. Aaron wrote as fast as he could. He had a label for each car. And for the riders in each car a label identifying the bearer as "parent" or "friend of parent."

Mr. Bradshaw was delighted by this flurry of activity. Everyone was busy. Everyone had a tag. The camp was a model of efficiency and order. That evening he presented the parents and campers with a treat. Following dinner we were invited to watch a film. As the light struck against the dining room wall I couldn't believe what Mr. Bradshaw called a treat. The film dealt with water safety. There were extensive scenes about mouth-to-mouth resuscitation and how to throw a drowning swimmer a life ring. Behind the scene was the sight of children cavorting in the water. White teeth glistening. Children running and jumping into the water. I hated these blonde-headed kids and their smugness. The film ended with a Red Cross demonstration of water ballet. Graceful legs poising above the water and then darting beneath its surface. Children kicking in unison toward the center of the pool to form symmetrical stars and flowers with their arms and legs. The film ended without applause.

That evening camp was quiet. There was no singing. Dominic didn't tell any Mafia epics. And those labels were like a hundred spying eyes. They were everywhere. Reminders of who we were and what our place was in the order of things. Late into the night I was awakened by a crash of ash cans and an erratic flashlight that shot right into my face. In a stupor I climbed out of bed and headed toward the noise. I thought one of the kids had gotten tangled up trying to go to the bathroom. The noise of crashing and thrashing about increased as I got closer. It was Mrs. Nelson; she was lying on the ground with this big smile and one upraised eye, her flashlight swinging wildly. She was totally inebriated. No, she was blind drunk. In her hand she had a dozen or so labels. She threw her head back and in a slur of perfection declared, "See here, I've got them . . . all of them." "Well, not quite," I thought, "but you've got the idea." I picked her up and we weaved together through the camp toward her cabin. Along the way she would sway to rip off a label here and a label there. I started helping her in this purge. She smiled and giggled at the sight of help. Together we did the deed.

DAY 8

Next morning everyone asked who had removed the labels. Even Mr. Bradshaw was missing. He was off on another fund-raising junket. There was speculation that the good camp fairy had made the visit. Spider was convinced it was the Green Hornet! Aaron voted for Mr. Clean. Martin speculated that bears did it. The questioning and hypotheses about our benefactor raged between breakfast cereal, fruit, and rolls. It's funny how heroes must always be bigger than life.

Like the surprise and wonder of finding the sky, revolution can't be planned. It happens when you least expect it. Its clerics are not bigger than life but humble and simple souls. Like the person next to you. Revolution is a Rosa Parks, who decides one day not to ride in the back of the bus. Or a navy nurse named Mrs. Nelson, who suddenly refuses to let her children be condemned to a label.

Throughout the hubbub Mrs. Nelson sat in a corner holding her head and nursing a cup of coffee. As curiosity crescendoed I informed these seekers of the truth that "I know who did it!" It was a pleasure to know that although I couldn't act like a rebel I at least could identify one if the chance presented itself. The time was now. I pointed deliberately to the corner of the room. Everyone looked and then looked back. "So who did it?" Spider inquired. I pointed again. "Not Mrs. Nelson," chided Benny. "Yes, Mrs. Nelson," I replied.

Mrs. Nelson was a genuine camp hero. It couldn't have happened to a nicer person. I'm not at all sure she remembered her gallantry but her legend spread unabated. From that moment she couldn't keep the kids away from her. You might say she was captured by good intentions. Kids would huddle around her proposing things to do. It was as if she possessed some kind of magic. Well, maybe she did. After all, she stripped those labels off all of us. She gave us back the chance to be children. To dream and play.

Day 10

Play we did. Some of the girls organized a dance. It was crazy. Beautiful. We all dressed up. The boys perfumed themselves with Wildroot and Dixie Peach. Martin got his rangy red hair into a ducktail. Benny and Thomas settled for the natural look. Spider had his hair slicked into a Rudy Vallee shine. Aaron had a crew cut that with the aid of Vaseline stood straight up. All three inches of it. The girls wore ponytails and lots of ribbons. For music we had Mrs. Nelson's slow records. Can you believe Frank Sinatra? For those into the twist we had the Chantells or some such group. We also had some down home country music and one record of the bunny hop. The dance started like every dance. Boys on one side of the dining hall, girls facing them. Three records played and no one moved. Janie, one of the girl counselors, joined hands with some of the blind girls and made a line. She started describing out loud what she was doing. There was a great squeal of "oh no's." Janie walked over to the record machine and put on her favorite country song. Back she sashayed to the waiting line of girls, broke into the middle of the line and shouted, "Here we go! Four steps forward. Four steps back. Turn around and slap your back." She was giving a spontaneous square dance call. I grabbed Martin and some kids in chairs and we followed Janie's call. Circled right. Turned around and said goodnight. Pretty soon the whole hall of kids and counselors was moving to Janie's call. Not all together, mind you. But moving. We were the dancingest moving fools you ever saw.

Once you start it's hard to stop. Janie called a Virginia Reel. She had the boys line up across from the girls, then peel off in couples and parade, wiggle, or wheel down the corridor of clapping, shouting kids. There was a commotion of jockeying to line up with the right partner. With our kids the chance to dance with a girl brought a mixed and surprising reaction. Benny B. would have nothing to do with this nonsense. He sped about the hall showing off to a diminishing audience. Martin had the dilemma of three girl-friends. They were his diving friends at the pool. He asked if he could "cut in" on the line so that he would have the chance to, as he put it, "share himself with the ladies." I promised to help him. Aaron, of course, had to dance with Mary. Thomas wanted to watch. Spider was courting his favorite girl counselor.

I don't think you could call what we did a classic Virginia Reel. What took place reminded me of kids on "Bandstand" doing that jive stroll as others stood applauding and moving up the line for their turn. For our kids the slightest turn of the shoulder or turn of the wheelchair was rewarded. Every dancer had his own style. They slipped, slid, and just had fun. By the end of the dance the kids and counselors were making up their own rules. Groups of four or five children and counselors would grab hands and come down the center of clapping contestants. Martin was last down. He had the biggest grin on his face I've ever seen. He also had three young ladies.

If the stroll was for the big kids, the bunny hop was for the kid in all of us. Everyone could do it. This was Benny's favorite. We formed a big conga line of wheelchairs and weaving bodies. With a hop hop hop or its equivalent the bunny hop began. Closing your eyes and listening to the screams of delight and exhilaration, you might imagine yourself in the heart of the old fun house at the beach in San Francisco.

Finally the big moment of the dance arrived. Janie asked for quiet. Then, with everyone at attention, she announced the crowning of the Camp Wiggin King and Queen. I knew it. I knew those girls would romanticize this occasion. No dance is proper without such goo. Benny and I were allies on this. Benny complained, "Oh heavens no." I agreed. Spider in typical good humor suggested in undertone, "Mr. Bradshaw for king." Like most King and Queen things I knew it was fixed. I knew who would reign.

I was wrong again. Mrs. Nelson was a perfect Queen. She preened and threw kisses to everyone. So who would be King? There was the traditional murmur and rustle. "The girl counselors, after consulting with girl campers, and the camp cook, proudly and with great honor proclaim the next King of Camp Wiggin to be . . . Aaron Gerwalski." "Who?" "Aaron Gerwalski." "That's Arid." "It's our Aaron." Even Benny was excited. "Our man Arid did it, he made it," he said. "Yeah, and he gets to kiss all the girls," added Spider. Aaron was a perfect choice. In grand style we wheeled him to his waiting throne and his Queen. She picked him up and gave him a big kiss. Bright red lipstick right on the forehead. Aaron was speechless, embarrassed and thrilled all at once. Buffeted by all this attention. Searching for a reason for this adulation, he turned to the assembly and, before he could speak, answers began to break their way toward him. "It's your hair, it can hold a crown by sticking to it." "Aaron, you're the best cook in camp." "Aaron, you're just neat." That last comment caught Aaron's need. He turned and smiled in the direction of the comment. His expression ignited the crowd into three cheers. Three cheers for the King and Queen of Camp Wiggin.

It's not easy being a king one moment and a child the next. Wheeling Aaron back to our cabin I couldn't see his face for the evening shadows. I could feel his body in the chair. He had his hands cupped over his face. He bent forward in his chair. Body shaking and quivering. Taking in quick gulps of air. Then pushing the air out in repeated sobs. Tears were streaming down his face as he turned in embarrassment from other campers. "I've never been a king before." Still pushing him slowly I responded, "Most of us will never be kings." Aaron continued, "But I'm so happy, why am I crying?" Before I could think of an answer he had another question. "Do kings cry?" I had an answer, "Yes."

That night camp filled with the shepherd chorus of "Cum-Ba-Ya." One cabin would start singing. Others would join in and then silently hold their voices and just listen to the others singing. We were at peace with the world. I thought I could hear each voice in the camp somehow held suspended by all the voices. And the soft singing of Benny and Spider. And what a marvel—Thomas singing faintly for the first time.

> Someone's singing, my Lord
> Cum Ba Ya
> Someone's praying, my Lord
> Cum Ba Ya
> Someone's singing, my Lord
> Cum Ba Ya
> Oh, Lord
> Come by here.

Why can't life be like this? Human beings in all their magnificence. Working to find that moment of pride. That one second of excellence at being alive. Hearing our singular voice held in harmony by the voices of those we love. The feeling of belonging not just to oneself but to the entire universe.

Camp days fled by like a tide leaving the sand. Each day seemed shorter. There were signs of anxiety. "How many days left?" was a constant question. The kids seemed to withdraw gradually but perceptibly into cocoons. I noticed that Thomas stopped talking and was slumping in his chair. Benny B. was racing about in a frantic way. He told me that if he stopped, the camp would end. The closing date was looming larger and larger. Mr. Bradshaw returned to camp to remind us that parents would arrive to be with us all day the upcoming Saturday. And final camp activities would end Saturday afternoon. He wanted the camp clean. So that was our fate. To spend the last three days of camp cleaning and waiting. I was asked to clean the pool. The place that we enjoyed the most was to sit unused.

Mrs. Nelson felt the brunt of this depression. Most of the girls returned their makeup and many children displayed symptoms of illness that marked their first few days at camp. Bed-wetting returned. Those kids on special diets who had been eating regular meals or Dominic's concoctions requested their pills again and wanted pampering. Mr. Bradshaw provided the final blow to morale when he informed us that he planned another water film for Saturday. There was no response to this suggestion. In desperation I asked if we could at least keep the pool open until Saturday so that we could demonstrate how many of the kids had learned to swim. "Mr. Jones," he said, looking right at me, "the pool is your responsibility. Just be sure it's clean by the closing of the camp on Saturday." There was still no reaction from the kids. Mr. Bradshaw left the room and the camp. In leaving he thanked and complimented us for being good campers and counselors. He was proud to be a part of Camp Wiggin. And knew the parents would be pleased on Saturday. No one moved.

3 DAYS TO GO

We sat in silence for what seemed like an hour. Finally Mrs. Nelson started walking around the room with her hands behind her back like a priest on a morning walk. We all watched her circle quietly and then come to a sudden stop. "Why don't we . . ." she said. "Why don't we put on our own water ballet? Put on an extravaganza. With costumes. And a story. Everyone can take part. We'll put on a show for the parents. Well, what about it? Do we sit on our duffs feeling sorry for ourselves or do we do something? I'll get reporters and they can film us . . ."

That did it. That was the trigger. Film. Reporters. These kids had never been news. Most had been family secrets. They had been observers. Now they had the chance to be performers. "Can we do it?" someone asked, and before anyone could answer there was a resounding "We can."

2 DAYS TO GO

We had two days to prepare for the Camp Wiggin Water Extravaganza. Mrs. Nelson came to the pool for the first time. She had on an old wrinkled bathing suit and white skin that piled about her. She was a brave lady. I don't honestly think she could swim. Armed with ignorance, a drill-sergeant voice, and lots of courage, she started directing what she called *The Acorn Pirate*. She had in her hands several pieces of paper that looked like a diagram for building the Great Pyramid.

With Mrs. Nelson's directions, materials from the craft center, and lots of work, the pool was transformed into a lagoon complete with pirate ship, palm tree, and exotic plants. And, oh yes, one native idol. The changing rooms at the end of the pool were painted to look like the side of a ship. Portholes replaced windows. The flagpole with its speaker became the mast of the ship U.S.S. *Acorn*. Probably the first pirate ship commissioned into the navy by an ex-navy nurse. A sail was fashioned out of sheets, and a Jolly Roger pennant was fitted out slightly below Old Glory. Next came the costumes. The inner tubes were made into floating islands of flowers. Safety belts became ballet skirts, pirate belts, and native war dress. *South Pacific*, look out!

1 DAY LEFT

With one day left we had our set. It looked beautiful, this rogue pirate ship sitting in the middle of Camp Wiggin. Now for the performance. Mrs. Nelson called everyone together. She divided us into pirates and natives. Good guys and bad. As for the script itself, well, that seemed still to be a mystery. Once into our roles we were given various options. We could be divers. Or racers. Or dancers. We practiced our separate parts. The divers sinking to the bottom of the pool, on cue, of course. The racers pushing their inner tubes across the pool in intricate patterns. The dancers practicing a kind of Tai-Chi on the pool deck.

0 DAYS LEFT

Saturday was the big day. The Camp Wiggin Water Extravaganza was about to begin. Everyone went right to the pool to hear Mrs. Nelson's final instructions and get into their costumes. Mrs. Nelson began talking, "Now, children, I'll read the story over the camp loudspeaker. All you have to do is listen carefully and follow my instructions." As if on cue, cars loaded with parents, brothers, and sisters of the campers started arriving. They parked and were immediately greeted by a welcome committee that plied them with flower leis and invited them to the pool area for a play to be performed by the campers and staff. Janie and some of the girl counselors had ridden into Santa Cruz the evening before and to everyone's enjoyment returned with boxes full of Antonelli Brothers begonias. They worked all evening making leis. The surplus flowers covered the pool in bright exotic colors.

Parents conditioned to strained greetings were delighted. Family children accustomed to pampering or resenting their handicapped brother or sister found themselves wishing to be in the play. You could see smiles flash across the faces of the hosts. Pirates and natives waving to their bemused families. The excited and curious audience was directed to take seats around the pool. Mr. Bradshaw was late to arrive. With a delegation of trustees behind him, he faced a play about to begin. There was only one thing to do. Join in like everyone else. Well, at least the pool was clean. It even had flowers.

Mrs. Nelson approached the microphone. Papers in hand, she started to narrate and direct our water epic. "Once upon a time, an ugly pirate—that's you, Mr. Jones—sailed his ship the U.S.S. *Acorn* in Camp Wiggin Lagoon. The pirates with Mr. Jones were a villainous lot. Well, look mean, you pirates. That's right. Stomp around. Show off your eye patches and swords. Shake your fists at the natives. Good.

"The peaceful natives of the lagoon were a powerful and beautiful people. They simply chided (that's make faces) and taunted the pirates.

"The pirates, angered at this show of disrespect, pointed to their skull-and-crossbones flag. Finally, the captain of the pirates stepped out on the gangplank. That's the diving board, Mr. Jones. (No one said pirates were smart.) The captain of the pirates, a ferocious braggart, declared that he came for the treasure in the lagoon and that nothing would stop him. To get the treasure, he challenged the natives to a contest. It would be his pirates versus the natives. May the best group win."

Given this order to act, I pranced about looking all the natives straight in the eye. Then I walked about displaying the muscles and strength of my fellow pirates. In silent movie fashion I was overly dramatic. I know, because the audience started booing. Most of the kids got the idea and started posturing and posing. Spider and Martin played natives. When I passed them I lifted my eye patch and gave a pirate wink. They laughed and in retribution shook their acorn necklaces in my face. Taunting and teasing I tried to encounter each of the pirates and natives. I paused by each player to make some kind of gesture or salute, giving everyone a chance to receive some applause and recognition. The audience was fantastic. They got the idea and warmly greeted each of the players. The stage was set.

"All right, Mr. Jones, that's enough," called Mrs. Nelson. "The story must go on. And so the pirates challenged the natives to a contest of strength and wisdom. The first event of the contest was the dive for treasures."

With this introduction, Mrs. Nelson pulled a box from the girls' dressing room and with a heave dumped the contents into the pool. It was the camp silverware. Every last knife, fork, and spoon. Returning to the microphone, Mrs. Nelson calmly continued her narrative chatter.

"Pirate and native divers went into the water to collect the treasure."

The divers entered the pool. There were the sinkers like Martin, who silently submerged and in a sitting posture on the bottom used their arms and legs to scoop up the booty. And there were the divers. Those kids who went down head first tracking down a single piece of silver. Of course the audience awarded each find with hurrahs. With almost all of the treasure collected and piled on the pool side, Mrs. Nelson continued her story.

"The treasure was taken to the native temple of Oh La where it could receive the blessing of the god Oh La. OK, you pirates and native dancers, you heard me. The treasure was taken to the temple. That's it. Good. Now the only way the god Oh La would release the treasure was with the satisfactory performance of the legendary water ballet."

Given this signal the pirate and native players who had practiced roving about the pool were placed in their respective inner tubes. From the various edges of the pool they kicked and splashed into the center of the pool, where they formed a large circle. Then with the orchestration of Mrs. Nelson the circle was pushed in a clockwise and then counter-clockwise maneuver. The audience clapped in appreciation. It was hard. Kids like Benny wanted to go fast, while kids like Aaron and Thomas were doing all they could just to keep afloat. Each had to show a great deal of tolerance.

The circle move was followed by the formation of a floating star. And then the division of floaters into two lines. It was the Virginia Reel on water. The gods must have been happy. As the water ballet ended Mrs. Nelson proclaimed that a final contest would mark the end of the water extravaganza.

"With approval from the god Oh La the treasure was to be given to the winner of a race between the captain of the pirates, that's Mr. Jones, and the best native swimmer of all time—Spider, the Unconquerable."

It was obvious from the corresponding boos and adulation that Spider was the odds-on favorite. To build up for the big race, some of the pirates and I did evil-looking dives. The natives countered with their own dives. (Actually we had several kids who thought big splashes were the only appropriate act for such a play.) With the completion of the dives, the race was about to begin. Mrs. Nelson began explaining how the contest would be fought.

"According to ancient tradition Spider would be allowed to start first. This swimming start is to offset the fact that the captain of the pirates is known to cheat and use the gangplank as a diving board. Are you ready? Will someone help Spider get ready. All right. On your mark, get set, go!"

In the midst of a great roar Spider was off. Surging and kicking with all his might. I watched carefully, trying to calculate when I should dive. I knew that a running dive even done with lots of wasted motion could carry me a fourth of the distance across the pool. I also knew that to Spider this was a race and it wouldn't be right not to go all out. With this in mind I gave a pirate yell and dove headlong after Spider. I came up and spotted Spider perhaps halfway down the pool. With exaggerated but sure strokes I quickly began to close the distance. I could hear the crowd yelling frantically for Spider. "Faster!" "Faster!" "Come on, Spider!"

Just a little past halfway I drew abreast of Spider. I hesitated, trying to think what to do. To roll over and back stroke. To dive underwater perhaps and swim the distance out of public sight. I was now a clear body length in front of Spider.

I heard a yell. I looked over at Spider. With a jerk he was out of the water. In fact he looked like a rock skipping over the water's surface. He was alongside of me and then past me. Faster and then faster. I started swimming with all my might. Spider was cutting across the water at an incredible speed. I couldn't catch him. The crowd was ecstatic. Like a one-sided tug-of-war the natives had tied a rope to Spider and in unison were now beginning to pull him down the pool. He was bouncing over the water toward the end of the pool. With all my might I couldn't reach the edge and stop this rush. Everyone was yelling. Just as Spider was about to be yanked right through the pool side, the rope went slack and he coasted to the side like a surfer on a wave. Spider had won.

The race, the summer camp, the companionships were ended. Quiet moments of goodbye. I was reminded of our first meeting. A silent exchange. Now it was taking place again. Children, the precious bond to life, were being passed from counselor back to parent. It was quiet. Benny rolled slowly by himself from our presence. Spider was passed from arm to arm. Martin walked holding my hand. He was leading. Thomas Stewart had to be carried. His eyes were a little older and sadder. Aaron wanted to push himself. Show his parents his strength and acorn necklace.

For many of the girl campers the farewell was of special significance. They had become young women. One carried a hidden crush. The word filtered to me like a breeze. Several girls broke from the goodbye with parents and hurried to the pool. I felt very embarrassed by this rendezvous. They pushed and prodded one of their members forward and then vanished. It was a close friend of Mary—the girl Aaron had given his necklace to. She was equally embarrassed yet demanding of the situation. She had enjoyed summer camp. Loved my voice and enthusiasm. Thought I was a good pirate. Wanted to know if I would write. Wanted to hold my hand. Touch my face. I held her hand very gently. She asked me if I would close my eyes. If I would be at summer camp next year. If I would say goodbye. With a kiss. I bent down and touched her lips with mine. I would be here. I would remember summer camp forever.

This unexpected moment took me away. I didn't even see the members of the Acorn Society leave. I think they knew and even approved. They understood and felt many things I would never comprehend. They were racers, mountain climbers, observers, and kings. And they were dying. "Most will not live past their teen years."

EPILOG

All the principal children in this story are now dead. Dominic and I kept in close touch with these children for five years. Dominic's connections with the Mafia turned out to be more real than story. With money from legitimate business and lots of volunteer help, Dominic and I conducted trips for these friends and an annual Christmas party. Thomas and Aaron died one year after summer camp. Spider was killed by a car the following year. Martin died in a car accident four years later. Benny B. was the last child to leave this place. Of all the children he was the only one to have a funeral. At the final service Benny's mother gave me a white envelope. Inside was a crumpled acorn necklace. She said he gave them to everyone he met.

Winning

Every basketball coach hopes to encounter a "benny" somewhere in his coaching career. A benny is one of those special kids who come along once in a lifetime—a kid who won't leave the gym until you've turned out the lights and locked the door. And after it's locked, he'll have fourteen ways and nine friends ready to reenter. He possesses all the natural skills and instincts of a great player: a desire to work hard perfecting the most elementary moves, and work even harder to help his teammates experience success. Perhaps that's the invisible quality that makes a benny. The unselfish willingness to share the art of basketball with anyone who cares to listen or participate in the game. Whatever that spirit is, it's the quality each coach looks for. It's the thing to build around and learn from. It's a winning season and perhaps a lot more.

As the basketball coach at Cubberley High School in Palo Alto, the likelihood of my finding a benny was slim. The students at Cubberley were white middle-class children of professionally oriented parents. For the most part, these kids mirrored their parents; they were striving to become successful at something. What that something might be was never made clear. Without an objective in mind, the striving became all-important. At Cubberley it meant getting in "advanced ability" groups, getting good grades, getting accepted into a good university. Getting ahead. Getting through school. Getting. There was little time for intensity or giving to any one thing. Especially a sport.

It turned out that I was wrong about ever finding a benny at Cubberley—it started when school integration came to Palo Alto. Black students volunteered to be bused from Ravenswood High School in East Palo Alto. Cubberley, as "host" school, received its allotment of twenty-three "guest" students. I waited anxiously to see if any athletes might be part of this group. Of course I was looking for a benny. Three days after the transfer students arrived, I called the first basketball practice.

The turnout was excellent. Our basketball program had been successful during the past few years, and it gradually became known that if you turned out, you would get a chance to play. The prospect of gaining some new players from Ravenswood added to the tension and excitement of the first practice.

As the players came out on the floor for the first time, I noted some familiar kids who had started on last year's team. With fluid movements they began the slow and graceful art of shooting their favorite shot, dribbling a few steps, and rearing up to take another shot. Rebounding and passing out to a fellow player. Reliving past plays. Moving to the fantasy of future game-winning shots. Eyeing the new players.

The new players clustered at the baskets on each side of the central court. They dribbled the available basketballs in place and watched the players moving on the center court. They didn't talk much and looked a little frightened. Then, as if on cue, they began to turn and shoot at the available baskets. They, too, had a private shot and a move to the basket. Soon the entire gym was alive with players mimicking against invisible foes and arching up game-winning shots. Another season was beginning.

Midway through this first practice, Cubberley High School basketball was introduced to Huey Williams. He came rushing into the gym. In fact, he ran around the entire court three times. He didn't have a basketball. He was just running. And smiling. Nodding his head to the dumbstruck players. He didn't speak a word—just smiled and nodded hello. By his third lap, everyone knew we had our first black athlete.

Huey Williams wasn't exactly the transfer student coaches dream about. He was short, about the shortest player on the club. With stocky frame and bowed legs and radar-like hair, he seemed like a bottle of soda water, always about to pop. His shots were explosions of energy that pushed the ball like a pellet. When he ran, he couldn't stop. He'd race in for a lay-up and, instead of gathering his momentum and softly placing the ball against the backboard, he would run straight ahead, full speed, ejecting the ball in mid-flight like a plane letting go a rocket. The ball usually slammed against the backboard or rim and careened across the gym. To say it simply, Huey was not a basketball player. He was something else.

Every player carries a personality to the game. That's part of what makes basketball so interesting, because someone's personality is directly reflected in the way he plays. Now, Huey brought with him a personality I had never seen before. He loved life, people, school—anything and everything. "Mr. Jones, how are you today?" he'd say. "Fine, I hope."

You had to agree with Huey. His view of the world was contagious. He always had a smile that burst out when you least expected it. "Mr. Jones, I didn't shoot too well, did I?" He'd be smiling, getting ready to shoot again.

As the first black player on our team, Huey was well received. After all, he didn't represent a threat to any of the white players. If anything, he was a puzzlement. How could anyone try so hard, smile so much, and play so bad? Weren't all blacks supposed to be super athletes? How come he doesn't know his place, isn't solemn, and I like him? You couldn't help but root for Huey and want to be around him. Carnegie and the "make-you-feel-good Zen folks" could take lessons from Huey. He was a good human being who shared his optimism about life with anyone who ventured into his path. A smiling Huey started every practice with, "We're going to win this whole thing, Mr. Jones. Just watch!"

I didn't share Huey's enthusiasm. It was the most unusual group of kids I had ever coached. In fact, the team really constituted three distinct groups. Huey represented one of these groups. This was a collection of five kids who had never played before. They couldn't shoot or dribble, let alone jump. Passing was iffy. When they were on the court my greatest fear was that they might run into each other. Although lacking skill, they personified Huey's faith and willingness to work hard. My God, how they tried.

A second group of kids on the team had played together the previous year. They were typical Palo Alto kids. I guess Chris Martin most exemplified the personality of this group. Chris was a class officer, good student, achievement-oriented, and serious about winning and, of course, playing. Chris just tolerated Huey and most everything else. His attention was on the future. Basketball at Cubberley was like the Pony League, Little League, and Junior League he had participated in so well. It was one more right step to some mythical big league called IBM, Hilton, or perhaps Standard Oil.

Chris knew all the lessons and skills of basketball. His jump shot was a picture-book example of perfection. He released the ball at the peak of his jump and followed through with his hands guiding the path of the ball as it slid into the basket. Chris's behavior might be described as that of a little old man—he was finicky at the age of sixteen. If things weren't just right, his voice would stretch several octaves and literally squeak. For Chris, things going just right meant a championship and of course a starring role. I liked and felt sorry for Chris at the same time. He reminded me of myself—a little selfish and awfully conceited, and extremely insulated from feelings.

A third group of kids making up the team could best be described as outlaws. Dave Warnock characterized this group. Whereas Huey had a reverence for life and Chris was busy controlling life, Dave seemed always to be on guard and challenging hell out of it. He was perpetually in trouble. Usually a team is composed of kids like Huey, who can't play, and kids like Chris, who have played throughout childhood. Kids like Dave rarely show up on a team. To have five kids like this on the same team was most unusual, if not intolerable.

Dave's style of life and play was outside prediction. Dave reminded me of a stork trying to play basketball. His arms and legs flailed at the air as he stormed up and down the court. His shots were what players call "watch shots." He would crank up the ball without facing the basket from some unexpected place and, yes, it would go right in— prompting the defensive player to say, "Look in the other

hand, you might find a watch." Dave was always a surprise
—a surprise if he showed up for practice and a surprise that
he stayed with it. In a strange way he was also a breath of
fresh air. He lived to the fullest. He didn't stop to explain his
actions. He just acted.

So there you have it. Not exactly a dream team. Five
kids charging around looking for the pass they just dropped.
Five kids straining for an expected championship. And five
kids who might not even show up for the game. The entire
team tilted on the verge of combustion. The kids who centered around Chris and Dave openly hated each other.
Huey and his troop of warriors became the grease that kept
the team moving together. Happy and delighted to be playing, they were oblivious to the conflict. In their constant attempt to mimic a Warnock pass or a Chris jump shot, they
inevitably made the effort look ridiculous.

Huey, with his intensity and honesty, put everything
in perspective. It was simply impossible to get angry or serious about yourself with Huey around. He had girlfriends
to tell you about, a cheer for a good play, a hand for someone who had fallen, and a smile for everything. And if all
that failed, he always had his "new shot" to show you.

Huey's enthusiasm was contagious, and it wasn't long
before everyone was working to help him and the other inexperienced players. Chris was telling players about the
right way to shoot. Dave was displaying one of his new trick
passes. I was working hard to teach defense. If you don't
have the ball, go get it. Don't wait for someone to put it
through the basket or even start a play. Go get the ball.
Chase it. Surround it. Take it.

We worked on how to press and trap a player with
the ball. How to contest the inbounds pass. Double-team.
Use the full court. Cut off the passing lane. Work together

with teammates to break over screens and sag into a help position. Work to keep midpoint vision. Block out. Experience the feeling of achievement without having the ball or scoring the winning point. Taking pride in defense.

The intensity and intricate working of defense was something everyone on the team could do, and something new for everyone to learn. Defense is something most basketball teams just do not concentrate on. It's the unseen part of the game. Working hard on the techniques of team defense began to slowly draw the team together with a common experience.

As for the offense—well, I taught a basic passing pattern, but the shooting was up to whoever was on the court. Chris and his group ran intricate patterns for the lay-up or percentage shot. Dave with his team took the ball to the hoop, usually after three dribbles and a confederate yell. Huey's team did their best just to get the ball up the court.

By the start of the season we had one spectacular defense and three offenses. In fact, I divided the team into three distinct groups. In this way everyone could play, and it confused the heck out of opponents. According to basketball etiquette, you're supposed to play your best five players. We played our best fifteen. You are also supposed to concentrate on scoring. We emphasized defense. Finally, a good team has the mark of consistency. We were the most inconsistent team you could imagine.

We would start each game with Huey's bunch. They called themselves the "Reverends." With their tenacity for losing the ball and swarming after it, plus their complete inability to shoot, they immobilized their opponents. The starting fives they encountered believed the intensity and madcaps of Huey's Reverends. By the time they realized they were playing against all heart and very little scoring potential, it was time to send in Chris's group. Chris's team called themselves the "A Train." That they were. Like a train, they methodically moved down the floor, executed a series of crisp passes, and scored. By this time in the game, Huey was smiling his all-knowing smile, and the coach from the other team was usually looking over at our bench in a state of confusion. Just as the opposing team adjusted to the systematic and disciplined play, we sent in Dave's "G Strings." Dave's team played with reckless abandon. They were always in places they weren't supposed to be. Doing things that weren't in the book. Playing their game.

By the middle of the season we were undefeated. Oh, I had to suspend Dave twice for smoking a cigar in the locker room, once for smuggling a girl onto the travel bus. And on occasion I had to remind Chris that I was the coach. But all in all the team was becoming a tight family—a disjointed group of kids were actually becoming friends. It was a joy to witness this chemistry. Huey's group gradually improved. They started believing they could beat anyone. The basketball still didn't go in the basket, but in their minds and actions they were "starters." As for Chris, he was actually beginning to yell for someone besides himself. And Dave, well, he didn't change much in an outward way. He was still frantic on the basketball court. It was off the court that he was becoming a little less defensive. He started telling me of things he wanted in life—things not that much different from those securities and accomplishments sought by others. In fact, it was something as simple as friendship.

Our first defeat of the year came not on the basketball court, but at the hands of the school superintendent. With twelve games already played, the superintendent declared that all transfer students were ineligible for interscholastic sports. It was a knee-jerk reaction to other

coaches in the league who feared we might "raid" Ravenswood High School of its top black athletes. No one worried
about our stealing away their intelligent students or class
leaders, yet that's just what we did. No one thought to ask
the students and parents how they felt. This was a coaches'
decision. Coaches who thought only about winning.

The superintendent ordered Huey off the team immediately. The announcement of this decision came not in a
telephone call or personal visit, but in a ten-word directive.
"No transfer students will be eligible for interscholastic
athletic teams."

The announcement came on a game day. The team
was already suited up and waiting for the last-minute game
plan. I read the decision to the team. They were stunned.
And angry. Ideas and plots for Huey's survival rang out
against the white-tiled dressing room walls.

Dave slammed his shoe against a locker. "It's a shitty
decision."

Chris agreed. "We can appeal. Let's go to the Board of
Education."

Dave snapped, "When--in three weeks?"

Everyone joined the argument. "Let's give Huey a
new number."

"Yeah, but can we also change his color?"

"We can play against ourselves, can't we?"

"Let's make up our own league."

In the din my own thoughts were welling up. How I
hated the way decisions were made at this school.

It happened every day in a hundred ways. The text-
book to use, the schedule to follow, the course to teach. At
no point in the schooling process was the teacher or student
allowed to make a decision and then be responsible for it.
Every day I and those around me were being robbed of the

chance to make decisions. It was like draining away life itself. Life must be tended daily—it can't simply be studied. Or mandated. Like basketball, it must be played the best way you know how. What do we teach when all we do is hand down and follow directives?

My thoughts were obviously slipping out of my mouth. I don't know when I started verbalizing my feelings, but I became aware of it as my whispers all of a sudden were audible in the now-silent locker room. As my personal decision became clearer, so did my pronouncement of it. "Huey's dismissal is wrong. It's unfair to defer the decision or obey it. I think we should forfeit all our remaining games. Huey is a part of this team. If you are willing to give other teams an automatic win over us in exchange for having Huey play, raise your hand." Fifteen players leaped to their feet. Dave was yelling. "Well, all right then, we've got a game to play." It was unanimous.

The players streamed onto the floor to begin their warm-up. I could hear a few rebel yells and even that high-pitched squeak of Chris's. Huey still brought gasps of surprise with his high-velocity lay-up. When he did his latest new shot—a sweeping, running hook—the assembled fans roared approval. Huey grinned and promised more. As the players finished their warm-up, the school principal came by to remind me of the superintendent's decision.

"Ron," he said, "I'm sorry about Huey, but he didn't start, did he? I mean, he hasn't scored many points for you, has he?"

"No," I replied. "Huey hasn't scored a point at all."

"Things will be different next year," he confided. I agreed.

As the game was about to start, the team huddled for final instructions. "Any afterthoughts?" I asked. "There is still time. . . ." We all were bundled together in a knot, hands thrust together in a tight clasp. Everyone looked up. Eyes all met. Every single kid was smiling. My God, I've got fifteen Hueys.

The horn sounded for the game to start. I took the entire team to the scoring desk and informed the league official, "We formally forfeit this game." The opposing coach, from Gunn High School, rushed over to see what the commotion was about.

"What are you doing?" he asked.

I told him of our decision. "That doesn't make sense— you guys are undefeated," he stammered. "We let two of our players go today."

"It's our decision," I explained. "We're here to play basketball, all of us."

And we did. All of us. Huey did his patented dash, Chris his jump shot, while Dave relied on surprise. It was a combination hard to beat. We poured in twenty more points than Gunn and, more importantly, displayed a constant hustle. Players ran to shoot free throws after a whistle. Ran to take a place in the game. Ran off the floor on being replaced. It reminded me of that first practice with this strange kid running around the gym. Perhaps we had learned more from Huey than we taught him. At the close of the game the Gunn coach stopped to comment, "Congratulations. You've got quite a team there." I reminded him that we had forfeited the game, that his team had won. He turned, "No, your kids won—they're a bunch of bennies."

———————

Dave Warnock is dead. Chris brought the message to

me. His father was a school official and he heard the news from the police. Dave had been at a party and had suffocated inhaling hair spray. Like a tape recorder erasing its contents, I couldn't think or act. Then, in forced flashes, I began to re-tread the past days. Searching for glimpses of Dave. His face. His antics. Was there something there? A warning. A plea. What did I miss?

The school community for the most part remained ignorant of Dave's death and its self-destructive cause. There were faculty murmurs—"That crazy kid. . . ." Other than these side glances at what had happened, there was no marking of Dave's death. Drugs and death are not part of the curriculum. It was improper to alarm parents. The school didn't stop its parade, even for a moment of respect or some other such platitude. Nothing. Everything as usual. Including basketball.

The team gathered for practice out of habit. The season actually had only a few days left. It had been a corrugated course. Our protest to allow Huey the right to play had sparked a boycott of all team sports. The boycott led to a change in the rules allowing transfer students to play with the condition that "due to the disruptions" no league championship would be awarded. It was okay with us. We declared ourselves champions. Actually, it was Dave's idea. Oh shit. It doesn't seem fair. Dave was a storm. He kicked and dared the world. And lost. Or did he? I don't know.

One good thing about sports is that you can lose yourself in physical exertion. Push yourself into fatigue. Let the body take over the crying in the brain. I informed the team that this would be our last practice. We would have a full-court scrimmage.

It was then that I realized Dave wasn't there. It's funny, Dave was dead yet I expected him to come prancing into the gym. The final trick on death itself.

Because we were short one player, I joined in the scrimmage. First, it would be Chris's bunch against Huey's team, and then Dave's group would play Chris's. I stood in for Dave. The play was strangely conservative and sluggish. Perhaps this measured play was in deference to Dave. Were we all letting our thoughts wander—just doing mechanical steps? Or was it a subconscious statement that Dave's life was errant and not to be emulated? Whatever, the play moved from one end of the gym to the other like the arm of a ticking clock. Up and down the floor.

It was Chris who broke the rhythm and the silence. Without warning, he sliced across the floor, stole a pass, dribbled the length of the court, and slam-dunked. Then, in an unexpected leap, he stole the inbounds pass. Taking the ball in one hand, he pivoted up a crazy sweeping hook shot. It was a "watch shot" if I'd ever seen one. Out of the blue, as the ball cut through the net, Chris erupted with a shrill guttural yell that pierced the stillness. It was a signal. The game tempo picked up—and became frantic. Everyone pushed to the maximum. Straining for that extra effort. Hawking the ball. Diving for a loose ball. Blowing tension. Playing with relaxed abandon.

It felt wonderful. The game was fierce. Everything learned in years of play was used. New moves were tried. I crashed for a rebound—elbows flying after a loose ball— and got it. Sprinted full tilt on a fast break. Yelled full voice as I fed Huey with a behind-the-back pass that he laid up for two. Everyone was moving as if driven by some accelerating spell of power and will. Everything went in. We could play forever. Play forever.

I pushed up a twenty-five-foot jump shot that was five feet beyond my range. It went in. Rushed to chase the ball. Try again. Seek the magnificent feeling of doing the undone. The unplanned. The unexpected.

The scrimmage raged on. The afternoon became evening, and still we played. The gym became fluorescent in the yellow light. Warm and wet. Racing now, back and forth. Exploding for shots. Playing the tough defense. Jumping over a screen. Blocking out. Back down for one more sensation of excellence.

My chest heaved for relief. My body throbbed. I couldn't stop playing. And didn't want to. Down the court. Set up. That's it. Feed the cutter. Fantastic. Now the defense. Keep low. Hell no. Take it away. That's it. Steal the goddamn ball. Now go. Fly.

I collapsed in a heap—legs simply buckled. I was shaking. Head not able to move. In slow motion, the team centered around my crumpled form. I'm all right. The air came rushing back into an empty body, giving life and movement. "I'm all right." Everyone was breathing hard, pushing out air and taking it back in. Grabbing their knees and doubling over. Letting the body know it was at rest.

Without any words, everyone gathered themselves. Then silently headed for the locker room and home. It's over. The scrimmage has ended. Practice finished. The season complete.

I slowly shower and dress, waiting for the locker room to empty. Walking through the silenced place, I stop to look and say goodbye. There is Chris's locker. A good kid. Hope his life goes well. He has changed and matured. Been a part of other lives. Huey's locker is still open. God, even his locker has a smile. What a person. I'll never forget. Dave's place. The cigar smoke is missing and so is Dave. I hate you for leaving us. I love you.

There is a sign that hangs over the exit from the locker room. It reads, "There Is No Substitute for Winning." Someone scratched out the word "Winning" and replaced it with another word: "There Is No Substitute for Madness."

There Is No School on the Sixth Floor

Last summer I found myself unexpectedly teaching school. My classroom was a hallway on a deserted floor of a mental hospital. The students were five adolescents hospitalized for psychiatric treatment and eight "street kids" paid to attend school. The school program was a part of an unusual experiment to prepare psychiatric patients for the real world.

The inner-city street kids were hired by the mayor's office as part of a summer employment program for disadvantaged youths. It was hoped that they might serve as therapeutic models for a peer group of severely disturbed young adults.

This introduction of the real world into the hospital setting was a unique situation. Most psychiatric hospitals attempt to help patients resocialize through companionship or volunteer community helper programs. But these efforts to ease the patient into the outside world take place *after* the patient is released. This care is comparable to "Here's the name of a friend, and here's a new coat," given to individuals leaving a prison.

Of course, it takes more than a new suit to catch up

with what's current on the outside. Especially if you're an adolescent. So a special summer school was initiated. Kids called "streetwise" were paid to help kids called "crazy" face the eventuality of leaving the hospital. It was an adventure-some idea.

The street kids were an amalgam of personalities. The self-proclaimed leader of the group was a young Chinese woman named Mary. Ideas shot from her like darts. As she talked, she literally painted words with her hands. Another kid named Johnny T. fielded Mary's enthusiasm with a gold-toothed smile. Johnny's radio and knit cap gave him away as a kid from South Hampton Street. He was one of those rare "tough" kids who could go anyplace.

Georgia was simply big. She was a large black woman who looked and acted as if she were in continual choir practice. She glided quietly into any setting and then anchored. She didn't say much, but she hummed a lot and you felt good being in her company. Alyce was also black, but she was different from Johnny T. or Georgia. Alyce's middle-class background kept showing. She was always acting to please, to find someone a chair, to share her latest accomplishment.

Whereas Alyce moved to accommodate the world, Vicki, Lisela, and Philip gave it color. They were from the city's Latino neighborhood. Their words overlapped and spilled into the air like machine gun fire. Staccato expletives about boyfriends, marriage, El Salvador, and a hundred incidents were ignored or absorbed by most of the kids. For Richard Lee, a tall Chinese kid, the salvo of words was something to dodge. With each surge of verbiage, Richard would wince and back up. Then spin and sit down, only to stand and turn again. Richard was a matador turning away from words and motion cast in his direction. Like a wind-up toy twisted too tight, you wanted to hold him for a minute and let the extra juice whirl away.

The final outside student was Ellen. She was the only white kid in the group. Shy and boyish in her heavy jeans and sweater, she was unique in one respect. Her younger sister was one of the psychiatric patients.

Although the city kids reflected a tremendous diversity in style, they held similar opinions about working with peers who were mental patients. They expected the patients to be "bedridden," "mentally retarded," and "unable to make sense." They felt the patients would be "talking about things that don't exist," "constantly running around tearing things up," and "always yelling like on TV." The greatest concern held by the city kids was of "being beaten up by a crazy patient."

The patients in the school program were also quite diverse. Leona was the group cheerleader. With her broad shoulders and her "rocker" walk, she looked like she was skating for the Bay Bombers. Leona was hospitalized for aggressive hostility. Her sister Ellen explained that Leona hit people, was always in trouble. That her stepmother couldn't stand her—"She could never come home." Leona's closest friend was Danny. Like most of the patients and outside kids, Danny was sixteen. He looked about eight or nine years old. His hair stuck up in the back and down over his eyes in the front. He looked like a Cub Scout in pursuit of merit badges. His body could run and jump over fire plugs, but his mind seemed stuck on questions of sexuality. Like a stuck record, he'd ask, "How long is your cock?" To girls, he'd smile and ask, "Can I squeeze your tits?"

Lynell was one patient who never heard Danny's question. Just as Danny's speech repeated, Lynell's every movement was ritualized. Her frail body would crank to a standing position, only to reseat, then stand again, and sit again, and stand again. Her walk was several steps forward, followed by a pivot and steps in another direction. Every action was methodically traced over and over, a process called "perseveration." A crusty webbing of dried tears covered Lynell's eyes like spider webs. Tobacco stains crawled over her fingers. Her uncombed hair and disregard for clothing made her look like an aged woman.

Of all the patients, "Zero" was the most mysterious. He looked like an average suburban senior high school student. In many ways, though, he was anything but average. Zero was an electronics wizard. Dying TV sets came to life under his care. At his command, hospital elevator doors would open to an exposed shaft. He could listen in on any phone conversation coming into the ward. And with little trouble he could vanish. In a ward charged with emotion he had found the secret of quietly blending into the scenery or exiting through an unnoticed door. So he lived in an electric world and played ghost to the real world.

Rella also hid from reality. Her escape took the form of silence. She never spoke. Periods of silence were interrupted by periods of severe vomiting. Her life swung back and forth from silence to physical illness.

Just as the city kids shared certain expectations about patients, the patients expressed a set of opinions about their counterparts outside the hospital. Generally they felt the city kids were "loud," "hard-looking," and "very dangerous." That "those people will pick on us," that "they'll make fun of us," that "they don't know about a hospital like this." And, "they'll probably hurt us, kick us and stuff."

They were two groups of kids separated by worlds of experience. Kids from city streets, called "disadvantaged," being asked to work with kids called "crazy." Both fearful of the other. Both willing to risk abuse and danger in order to attend an unusual summer school on the sixth-floor hallway of a hospital. What happened when these two groups actually met was the basis for some unexpected learning. Some surprises. And a new definition of the word "mental."

School didn't exactly start with the pledge to the flag. In fact, we didn't have a flag, much less desks or books. What we did have was a huge billboard depicting a fanciful spaceship. It seemed like a natural introductory activity. We had a roll of tape, a paper billboard, and lots of arms and legs. The perfect educational plot. City kids and patients would meet each other—help each other—and share in the success of covering an ugly wall. Everything about this plot was perfect except for one thing. The tape. It stuck to everything but the wall.

Like learning, chaos can start quite innocently. In the case of the billboard, it started with Georgia.

Georgia used her massive size to tear delicate pieces of tape and affix them to the floor. They stuck up like grass. Actually, it was Mary's idea. She directed everyone to start taping the edges of floored paper. Johnny T. smiled. Alyce tried to help by passing tape to waiting hands. It stuck to her and those she touched. Vicki and Lisela rolled the taped paper against the wall and continued talking. Richard and Ellen dutifully continued taping.

And the patients? Well, they were really needed. They greeted the sight of the street kids struggling with tape as a worthy adventure. Leona used her roller derby strength to hold up the top of the billboard. Danny used the moment to chase after Mary. His pursuit left a trail of sticky tape. Alyce stopped handing out tape. She sat down. Found herself taped to the floor. And was too embarrassed to get up. Lynell, the patient of a thousand directions, held out a corner of paper and wouldn't let go. Rella just watched. Zero gave a nervous laugh and disappeared into an empty room. Johnny T. and Philip formed a human ladder to hold and tape the upper edges of the billboard. They demanded more tape.

Bodies pressed and sprawled against the paper. Tape was passed from hand to hand to wall. Tape hung like fringe from shirt sleeves and grabbed at unsuspecting feet. It did everything but hold the paper against the wall.

Suddenly the paper spaceship unraveled like an avalanche. It buried its tormentors. Covered them like a tent. No one escaped the falling paper and its tangle of tape. In slow motion Johnny T. and Philip cascaded downward with the roll of paper. For a moment there was nothing but silence, then a giggle, followed by yelps of laughter. Feet kicked to get free of the paper maze. Bodies scrambled into a stance. Tape was everywhere. It would take another hour to put up the paper spaceship. But it did get up. One spaceship flying through the hallway. It signaled the start of summer school. A fragile alliance between street kids and inside patients had begun.

The impact of street kids on patients was immediate and dramatic. In the first few days of school, Danny was the subject of all our attention. He was in love. In love with Mary and Georgia and Alyce and Vicki and Lisela and Leona and Lynell and Rella. He displayed his passion by squeezing girls' tits. Often by a surprise maneuver. He would spring from a hiding place or run full tilt down the hall to embrace his victims.

The girls went bonkers. They threw words of warning, "Cut that out!" Then words of consequence, "I'm going to smash you if you touch me again." Danny took these taunts as encouragement. Mary finally explained—"It's not

that we don't like you, it's that we don't like what you're doing." Danny greeted Mary's explanation with a smile. He
put his hands over Mary's breasts and tickled with his fingers. Mary grabbed his hands and pulled them softly to his
sides. And held them there as she continued, "Boys don't
treat girls that way. My boyfriend doesn't treat me like
that!" And so it went. Danny received daily doses of street
etiquette. The message finally got across.

We were doing some improvisational drama. Each
student was given a statement on a piece of paper saying,
"You are robbing a train" or "You are washing a car." The students were asked to find others holding a similar statement—
and they were to conduct this search without using words.
Danny started to follow Mary, then suddenly stopped. He
became busy writing on slips of paper. In the midst of people acting out the robbery of a train or washing cars, Danny
circulated his directions. Georgia showed me the result of
Danny's labor. He was distributing his version of the assignment. It read, "Grab Danny and give him a kiss." Mary reacted by walking straight at Danny. She didn't speak or hesi-
tate. She kissed him gently. Danny had met the real world
and found a way to touch it without being hit in the face.

By the second week of summer school, Vicki and Lisela institutionalized the idea of giving. They called it Kriss
Kringle. Everyone put his or her name in a hat and then we
drew names. I pulled Georgia. In the week that followed, it
was my Kriss Kringle responsibility to give Georgia a gift
each day. I was not allowed to tell anyone who I had drawn.
At the end of the week we were to tell that secret. Gift-
giving graced our presence for five days. I arrived one morning to find that my Kriss Kringle had prepared me a complete breakfast. An unnamed poet posted his work as a gift
for everyone. Alyce received a lace fan. Someone gave Dan-

ny a copy of *Penthouse*. Lynell, the patient who looked so feeble, was given a bright ribbon for her hair. Johnny T. got a supply of batteries for his radio. Rella, the girl who was almost catatonic, found a daily supply of chocolate chip cookies. She began to share them. Several girls were supplied with perfume and makeup. Patients unaccustomed to using cosmetics and trying to look good suddenly started coming to school in eye shadow and traces of rouge. Lynell wore her new hair ribbon with a beautiful cameo. The cameo was something her grandmother had given her. Something she had kept in a bottom drawer. Something she now wore with a glow of pride.

Richard, the shy outside kid, took a Polaroid picture of Lynell and her finery. Lynell smiled. It was the first time I had seen that. The photo caught that moment. Lynell looked with disbelief at the photo, then walked away without saying a word. In a few moments, she lurched back down the hall. She was walking in a steady gait. That's right. She was walking in a deliberate direction. No turns. No steps forward and back. She walked straight to Richard. Then she spoke, "What's 'photogenic' mean?" Richard answered, "It means you're beautiful." Lynell smiled broadly. "The nurses downstairs said I'm photogenic." Richard was as pleased and as rewarded as Lynell. The chemistry between street kid and patient was beneficial to both.

Perhaps the greatest gift provided by street kids was the freedom they offered. Prior to the summer the patients had not been allowed on field outings. For many patients this meant they had been confined to the hospital ward for over a year. Midway through the summer, Mary argued for control of our budget. It was given. With the money, the students planned an outing to a roller rink. I was surprised to find that the hospital had no outing policy, and therefore had no outings. When Mary pursued this matter she found that the hospital insurance regulations prevented our use of private cars. Or buses. Or taxi cabs.

Mary found a solution—a form of transportation not stipulated in the insurance policy. She argued, if it's not in writing, it must be permissible. Her solution was a joy to all. She rented a large black limousine from a local mortuary. On the designated day for our roller skating trip, we found a slinky Mercedes limo waiting in front of the hospital. Mary ushered everyone into the limousine. Three nurses volunteered to go along. The psychiatric ward had its first field trip. And much more.

It turned out that Lynell, the girl who could barely walk, could roller skate. And Rella, the patient who never spoke, asked to go along. We had rented the entire rink for ourselves. The manager was delighted with his early morning customers. We zoomed about. Johnny T. was silk on wheels. Leona, her sister Ellen, and Georgia inched around the arena wall. Alyce could skate backwards. Mary, Vicki, Lisela, and Richard formed a whip that sent both ends crashing toward the middle. Most of us practiced graceful falling and surprise stops.

After a few minutes of skating, it became obvious that the manager liked us. From his booth at the end of the rink, he announced, "All right, ladies and gentlemen, I have a special surprise for you today—haven't done this in years— we're going to do the Lindy." A scratchy record came on. It sounded like a rhumba. The manager placed a bar in the middle of the rink. Our mission was becoming clear. "All right now," the loudspeaker cracked, "everyone up for the Lindy Low. How low can you go?"

With the manager waving encouragement, we skated kamikaze style toward the bar. The object was to duck under the bar and still stay on your skates. Johnny T. whizzed through with a graceful dip. Danny and Richard approached the bar in a gale of laughter. They both crashed through it. Alyce skated full speed at it and then ducked into a ball that flew under the bar in a blur. Everyone clapped. Georgia and Leona walked up to the bar in a stagger, grabbed it, and walked through. More clapping. Danny raced toward the bar, again, and slid under like a baseball player sliding home. Zero circled the rink, then dashed at the bar. At the last second, he stooped into a crouch. The crouch exposed his invention; Zero had tied skates to each hand. They worked like the landing gear of an airplane. He swooped under the bar, riding on four roller skates and a grin. His victory was contagious. Everyone was rooting for everyone else. We enjoyed the greatest freedom of all—play.

Exhaustion finally took its toll. Skates were gingerly pulled off and stuffed back into boxes. Rear ends were rubbed. The candy machine assaulted. As we were leaving, the manager of the rink moved to hold open the door. He was obviously pleased at the day's events. In a final gesture of goodbye, he declared, "Nice group you have here— you're good kids, not like those crazies that usually come here." A secret smile traveled across twelve faces simultaneously.

Summers don't end. They tuck away someplace in your memory. And wait to be recalled. For me, this was a special summer. It was one of those summers when your ideas about things get tested and sometimes change. This had been a summer of change. At the close of the school, I asked the patients how they felt about their counterparts from outside the hospital. They responded: "I thought they'd make fun of us, but they didn't. . . ." "They don't feel sorry for us. I like that." One patient acknowledged, "I still feel embarrassed in front of them about being in the hospital." The same patient then summarized how the patients generally felt: "We all blend together; they don't seem all that special."

As for the outside kids, their opinions about the patients also changed. They noted that patients come across not as crazy and destructive, but as quieter, less confident, and more reclusive than their community peers. They expressed surprise that the differences they expected to encounter were not as radical as anticipated: "They seem normal to me." "The kids are different, but they're not bad." "I've kinda enjoyed their company." Perhaps Johnny T., with his gold tooth and constant smile, summed it up best: "They're a little mental—you know, like me."

The High Diving Board

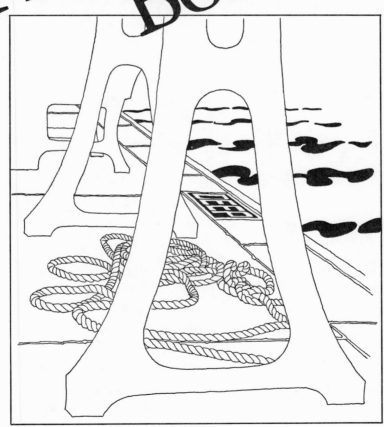

The high diving board is the first thing you see when approaching Forest Swimming Pool. It stands like a guard tower over the fence-enclosed pool. I've been watching this high diving board and the activity that surrounds it for thirty years. As a child I couldn't wait to go off that precipice. When my turn came I did the best cannonball possible for someone wearing surfer trunks and not wanting to get his hair wet.

In those days we called the cannonball "wicked." That's if you did it just right. If you timed it perfectly you could curl your body and smash into the water a few inches from the pool's side. The closer you came to the side the better, because you swamped the girls who always hung on the pool railing. Girls who always asked you to try just one more.

Today I sit at the edge of the pool and watch my daughter enter the shallow end of the world. Soon she will follow the slant of the pool and venture into deep water. And I suppose she will also hear the call of that high diving board. No one can avoid its presence.

The high diving board. This is where things start. If

the performers on the high dive pierce the water like arrows, then that's what is copied in the deep end and tried in the shallow end. If the holders of the high board wear cut-off jeans, you can bet that cut-off jeans will be the uniform of the younger swimmers. The high diving board. This is where style and duty are set. Of course, in this water world the style setters are the young about to become old. Water butterflies spiraling and glancing into the light.

On this day, like all days before it, the young were practicing their art. These teenagers held time in their arms. They were on center stage, masters of the pyramid and the secret of flying. Today the boys were wearing layered garb. Boxer underwear showed beneath their outer trunks like some new flag. Every motion of this young guard was practiced significance. Even the act of getting out of the water was ritualized. They popped from the pool like someone jumping a fence, then threw their long heads of hair backward and forward, sending out plumes of moisture.

These underwear divers were somehow different from the ones who came before them. They seemed to attack the board as if trying to crush it. With violent thrust they crawled into the air, arms and legs grabbing invisible hooks. Twisting and contorting, they plummeted downward. At first they seemed out of control. Then, as if programmed, each diver followed a given course. One leg was pointed down and the other was pulled with both hands tightly against the chest. The falling body resembled a snake—hips to the side of the leg entering the water, head and shoulders pulled in the opposite direction. Each entered the water like a corkscrew, and the water exploded upward. The splash seemed higher and more violent than any cannonball or kamikaze crash. A percussional "thud" followed the upturned water as it drenched the onlookers.

The girls at poolside screamed for more. Adults looked on, remembering the day they climbed the sky and broke the water. The younger children watched intently. Younger boys wore their boxer underwear under their store-bought swimsuits. They yelled "Can-opener" and mimicked those who dared the high board. Younger girls yelled "Gross" and waited for the day they would be splashed.

At first I didn't notice the old man standing next to the high dive. In fact, I don't know how long he had stood there. Old men usually stay away from the high diving board. But there he was, standing erect, holding on to the ladder with one hand. He was wearing slippers and a white terrycloth robe. In thirty years of watching the high diving board I had never seen anyone dressed in robe and slippers.

The young men didn't seem to see him at all. In their surge to the top of the ladder they splashed water on the old man and jostled around him as if he were some part of the apparatus. A few of the younger children waited patiently behind the old man and then realized he wasn't in line but merely watching the action from the board. The man in the white robe seemed mesmerized by the depth-charge splashes caused by the young men. He stood for an hour or maybe more, judging the intricate form and balance required to do a can-opener. How the body must twist upon hitting the water and how the extended leg must sit under the body at impact and the pull of the arms to arch the back. The old man watched as, over and over, the young turks performed their water explosions. We all watched.

The young men crashed closer and closer to the side of the pool. Waves of water were pushed into the air. The smaller children were driven from the pool by the increasing bravado and daring of these high-flying divers. Perfection was close at hand—the perfect entry into the water, as close to the side as possible. The angry propulsion of water into the air, so high that the diver can push to the surface and be drenched by water he had sent to the sky. Young men raced to climb the ladder and try again, to hurl their bodies into the perfect trajectory. A rhythmic beat of bodies flying off the board and bombing into the water held the pool captive. Observers—young and old—held their breath and moaned approval with each successful crash. The young men responded by throwing their heads back, placing themselves in an aura of water. They raised their arms in the air signifying a triumph over the water. The water was being beaten into the air by human endeavor.

Then, abruptly, a voice drowned out the water's sounds.

"Hey, what are you doing?" one of the young turks yelled, pointing upward. "Get off the board—you're going to hurt yourself!"

The old man was climbing to the top of the high dive tower. One of the young men hurried up the ladder, reaching for the old man's arm. He grabbed the sleeve of the white robe, and it slid off the old man and landed in a puddle at the base of the tower. The lifeguard, suddenly aware of the drama on the high diving board, blew his whistle and gestured for the old man to climb down.

Attention fixed on this frail figure at the top of the tower. He seemed so alone and out of place, yet somehow determined. He tugged on a black jockey-style swimsuit that glistened against his pale skin. He walked carefully to the edge of the diving board. The board bounced softly with each of his steps, then became still as the old man rolled his arms as if to pump air into his body.

This confident gesture calmed the lifeguard and served as a magnet. Everyone was watching this old man on the high diving board, wondering what it was he wanted, what he would do. Was he going to try a can-opener or some last plunge?

"He must be drunk," an older woman offered. "Why doesn't he sit here like the rest of us? He's going to hurt himself!" she continued to explain.

The man in the silk swimsuit stood on the edge of the diving board—now motionless. An unusual silence weighed in the air. Everyone turned to look at this figure balanced on the end of the board. A collective gasp pulled the air from the board as the old man bent his legs and in slow motion sprang into the air. The old man arched parallel to the water. He hung suspended above the board like some glider. Arms spread wide. Head held up. Chest pushed out. Back cupped like a bow. Legs pinned together. Toes pointed. At the pinnacle of his jump he began to fall toward the water. Still he held that position—flat against the air. At the last second the old man pointed his head and arms downward and sliced into the water. His straight body caused hardly a ripple. There was no customary expulsion of water or sound of water and body compressing against each other.

When the old man broke to the surface the pool-side audience was cheering. Old ladies and young children were clapping and yelling congratulations. Comments and speculation followed the old man as he picked up his wet robe and walked slowly along the pool side toward the gate. As he passed me I noticed that the lady who had labeled him drunk was standing and whispering, "Bravo, bravo." I watched as the old man walked through the gate. At first I didn't think he would even turn around. But he did—just for a moment. He turned and looked in the direction of the high diving board.

The young men in underwear trunks were reclaiming the tower. They pounded on the board, sending out the sound of firing cannons. Then the first underwear flyer took to the air. I looked quickly to see if the old man was watching. He was. And if the young man on the board was aware of the old man. He was. The young man banged into the air. Higher than anyone had gone. Feet downward, he curled one leg under his body and grabbed the other with one hand. With the free hand he gestured defiantly with an upraised middle finger. That solitary finger scratched the sky on its downward trace, then disappeared in a current of water.

The body of the young diver crashed into the water with a thunderous convulsion. I wondered if the young man was all right. A jaunty flip of the head and spray of water from his long hair announced his well-being. And triggered a torrent of other underwear divers. Now they sailed into the air and into the water in flights of two, then three, and four. The high diving board was theirs. The young men paraded their explosive skill. The girls screamed. Again and again the young men slammed into the water. Buoyed by their art and their importance, they played and relaxed around their board. They chided the younger boys who tried to duplicate their feats. Sometimes they offered advice, or simply behaved as bullies. Arrogance is the right of those who own the high diving board.

In the midst of this celebration no one seemed to notice a small boy about nine years old go off the board. After all, it wasn't a significant event—just one little kid going off the board surrounded by older, more interesting, better divers. For the underwear swimmers this skinny kid didn't warrant attention. There were more important, more familiar things to notice and praise. So the swimmers in underwear suits just didn't see the small boy. Didn't see him walk precariously to the end of the board. Or note that he didn't do the customary bounce on the board. When he went off the board he didn't aim his feet downward like all those around him, or make his body into a fist. The small boy swept his arms sideward and hovered in the air for a second. For that moment he flew suspended by the air. Head up and chest out. Back arched. Legs together. With a downward thrust, he entered the water with his hands and arms clearing the way for the rest of his body. There was no expectant splash. And no one noticed the small boy's smile as he pulled himself from the pool.

I looked quickly over my shoulder to see if the old man had witnessed this sight. He was gone. And when I looked to see if any of the young underwear divers had cared about the event, I found them too busy and too delighted in their own presence to see or care about the achievement of a small child. As for myself, I kept my vigil of the high diving board. There were more children that day trying the new dive. And there would be more tomorrow.

The Last Meeting

"To protect your balls, stuff gym socks into your underwear. Right here, up front, where it will do the most good. Vaseline applied to the face is also a good idea. If you feel the sting of gas, don't rub at it. Keep your hands away from your eyes. There will be cold water at the first aid station. This is your bail number. Write it on your arm or the back of your hand. It's important. . . ."

The classroom was filled with seventy high school students. It was eight o'clock in the evening. I had been teaching all day and coaching the basketball team most of the late afternoon and early evening. Now it was my turn to counsel and supervise the student club called USM, or United Student Movement. What a joke. I was the youngest faculty member, so the principal assigned me this job. Maybe he knew that no one else would take the job, or hoped that I would quit after a few of these late-night meetings. Then he could disband the club, contending that they couldn't find a faculty sponsor. Whatever the reason, there I was in the midst of a revolution.

Like most revolutions, this turning point didn't spark from a vacuum. It had been rumbling toward its climax for years. You simply couldn't get out of its way. It turned you inside out, forcing you to face your true being—to make decisions that you would like a lifetime to think about.

I had been attending meetings like this for months. Now it was suddenly different. There was no debate or abstract theorizing. The purpose of this meeting was to organize an attack on the Oakland Induction Center. To declare and wage war against the United States of America. By the end of this meeting everyone in attendance would have to ask a critical question. Do I have the will and strength to throw my life against a government of which I am a citizen? Declare my cause so just that it may warrant the destruction of life itself? In the moments of preparation I looked closely at the "down jacket" revolutionaries and the events that imprisoned us.

I hated being in this position. Enjoyed life too much to put it up for grabs. What a box. The Vietnam War was vile. I often cried and shook with anger, just thinking about it. It had to be stopped. But me, why me? Where is the rest of the school faculty? Not one of them even knows of this meeting. And if they did, they would stay away. Where are the parents of these kids? How come children have to bear the moral weight of this nation—throw themselves at the war machine? How many children must be sacrificed before it stops? It's so easy to walk away. I don't even like these kids. They are brash and demanding, arrogant and proud. I wonder if they are scared. Shit, I don't think so. I hate and admire these kids in the same breath. We have been through so much. I've learned from them things that can't be talked about or read in a book.

We were meeting in the typing room. It was always the same group of kids. For two years we had been in each other's company. I had battled with them as much as with the school administration, trying to give some sanity to the issue of student rights. As combatants we came to know each other in an almost intimate way. It was a strange relationship. I don't honestly know what kept the interaction alive. We all disliked the Vietnam War, but that was something many people shared. No, the tie was something else. Perhaps it was an unspoken fascination. I was intrigued by the righteousness of their struggle to speak and organize on campus. And fascinated by their determination, stamina, and ability to bring about social commitment.

As for their interest in my presence, it was probably based on the reality of a need for a faculty sponsor. Without a sponsor a student club couldn't exist; it couldn't call meetings or use school facilities. The strongest tie between us didn't exist at the start but grew steadily as we shared increasing pain and hope, as we watched each other change under the pressure of an unrelenting struggle. We became witnesses to our own political growth. Saw in each other the trial of living a just and good life. Saw the anger, the frustration, the wall-to-wall waste in America that was pushing us like a time bomb toward some suicidal decision.

For some, this meeting would bring an end to the pain. A chance to turn back. Take a rest. Watch and learn. For others, it would mark the beginning of a new struggle, this time using physical force in place of words. Everyone in the room just about knew the actions that each would take. In this premonition there was a certain amount of sadness. For some the battle would be over. Their friendship and love would be missed, their ideals lost.

Of all the kids in the room, a few stand out. They will always stand out. Doug Monica, with his round, choir-boy face, was the parliamentarian and group historian. He was a little chubby. A shock of thick black hair brushed off his face. Dark eyes that were never still. Traces of Mexican ancestry in his rounded features and broad mouth. Doug was always a little bit nervous and a little bit suspicious. Depending on whom he was talking to, his language would slip from a Chicano-studded rhetoric to a suburban know-it-all. He like to argue and debate verbally. And was good at it. In fact, he hid his dislike for his middle-class upbringing with a constant flow of working-class history and revolutionary theory.

Doug had been head of Junior Statesmen and knew the mechanics of debate and Robert's Rules better than anyone. I mean anyone. Doug knew parliamentary procedure so well that he used it to demonstrate its ineffectiveness. If someone started making motions or holding the floor, Doug would unleash a flurry of words, binding the group in an inescapable web. He only had to do this demonstration a few times before the group voted to outlaw all rules of convention and replace them with a single mandate. "Anyone and everyone can speak at any time. No action shall be taken by the group unless everyone agrees to the action." It was called "coming to consensus." Whenever the group launched into one of its consensus-seeking forays, Doug would lean over to me and say, "Mr. Jones, now that's democracy! That's how all institutions should make decisions."

A constant companion of Doug was Sue Garret. She was extremely attractive—tall and stately with a look of elegance—and usually ended up being crowned student princess of something or other. I don't know what bond existed between Sue and Doug, but it seemed unyielding. They were always together. Doug, with his short, choppy stance, and Sue, with her tall, graceful posture. Doug being sometimes repugnant and always abrasive; Sue being attentive and always gracious. Whereas Doug would demand an action with, "Mr. Jones, we have to . . ." Sue would say, "Mr. Jones, don't you think . . ." Sue got her way. She was a brilliant tactician and doer. While others moaned about not having a mimeograph machine or meeting place, Sue was always on her way to successfully talking a minister out of some paper or a landlord out of some building. While most people would talk about action, she was the force behind its happening. While most seemed continually depressed by events, Sue was working every moment to change events.

Let me tell you a brief story about Sue. One evening the students planned to show a film series on the Vietnam War. They had been denied use of a school room at the last moment and were desperate for an auditorium. More than 200 people were already waiting at the high school. It was six o'clock and getting cold. The films were scheduled for six-thirty. Police cruising the school like gnats against a bare light bulb made any attempt to break into the school out of the question.

While most of the students were cursing the police and school officials, Sue was announcing that she had found a place to show the films. It was the parking garage of a commercial building. She pointed to a building within walking distance. It was perfect. There was an elecrical out-let for the projector and even a white stucco wall that could serve as a screen. The audience moved into its new theater. Boxes were taken from nearby garage bins for seats and jackets were spread over shoulders and into heaps to pro-tect the gathering from the cold. Oh, it was pure revolu-tionary masochism. The people huddled together, snuggling against each other for warmth. For once things were work-ing without controversy.

Well, almost. Two-thirds of the way into the film I heard a shrill Chinese shout. At first I thought it was someone giving a revolutionary salute. But the shrill continued. The crowd turned to hush the yelling, but it kept on. In desperation I stepped over sprawled bodies to see what the commotion was all about. Making my way to the entrance of the garage, I saw a small Oriental man dressed in pajamas covered by a flopping overcoat. He was yelling at the projector to stop, shaking and talking in Chinese and then in English. It was obvious that he was confused and mad. Mad at the film, I thought. No, mad at the fact we were using his building. His building! My God, he was the landlord. A police car wheeled down the street at the very moment of my discovery. Being now in a complete frenzy, the landlord lunged at the police officer, spewing an unintelligible mixture of words and gyrations. The policeman looked at me and then at the landlord, trying to put some sense into the scene. The old man was now poking the policeman with his finger. This broke the concentration of the officer and he turned angrily. "Here, let's get you home," he commanded. And in a moment he had the old man by the collar and inside the patrol car. Down the street they drove. I raced back into the garage. "Sue, did you get permission for this place?"

"No," she replied. She didn't say another word.

With the end of the film Sue stepped in front of the crowd and explained about the arrest of the landlord. The political jargon of "Right on" and "Down with the landlord" greeted her announcement. Sue stood there shaking her head no until the clamor quieted. Then she spoke, "We can take this building but it's people we must win. The landlord is not our enemy." She then asked for contributions to rent the garage.

Three weeks later the landlord showed up on campus. He was asking for Mr. Jones. I was quite worried and in the process of dreaming up apologies when we met. To my surprise and relief, he was smiling. In broken English and Chinese he explained how the police had taken him and given him a brisk warning not to go outside in his pajamas again. He laughed, recalling this moment. Here his building was being used without permission by hundreds of people and the police were concerned about men in pajamas. He then went on to describe how this lovely young lady had paid the next day for the use of the garage and apologized for not telling him of its use. That he and this young lady had talked for hours about China and what was happening there. Then he grinned and shook my hand several times. I hadn't time to say a word. In leaving, he turned and offered, "Please use the garage if you need it—no rent the next time. Just clean up, okay?"

If Doug was the group's theoretician and Sue its organizer, Mike Fox was its spirit. Just thinking of Mike Fox brings a smile to my face. What a character. Mike was Bob Dylan with a twitch. He was always in motion. Fists working against the air, he spit out the need for struggle against the war and the culture that fostered it. His wrath spread against the schools and their sandpaper treatment of vital issues and people. He riled against passive resistance. Demanded a constant struggle for personal and social freedom. I can't remember Mike ever being still.

As a matter of fact, I can't remember Mike ever being in class. No matter where you walked on campus, the chances were good that you'd find Mike with a small cluster of kids, talking away like a machine gun. "You know what school is teaching you?" he'd start up. "To be good niggers. That's right, do what you're told. Get ready to be good secretaries, technicians, and consumers. That's it, go to school, then to work, then to some great reward in heaven.

You might get a gold watch. Look out, there! No talking along the way. No questions. That's right, just keep moving. Get good grades, work for the man. Kill for peace, learn to hate. Hate yourself. . . ."

Mike had an audience whenever he stopped to speak. I've never seen anything like it. He could hold the attention of bikers, dropouts, and college professors. Like a comet, his words scratched across the surface of the brain. His ideas were searing, unorthodox poetry. Things unheard and unthought of. He made you look at yourself and things around you in a fresh way—to decry the fact that you were motionless without cause or reason. Seeing Mike work provided a vision of what it must have been like to be in the presence of a Fred Hampton or Leon Trotsky. Mike could have been a super athlete, rock star, or brilliant scholar. He chose to fight for freedom.

Doug, Sue, and Mike were not alone in their student army. Perhaps another sixty or so kids held similar attitudes. They represented a cross section of the school population. They were musicians, scholars, slow learners, and fast learners. Some were heavies, into carrying guns. Others were comedians who used their wit to express their will. Still others were sullen or quick to temper. In combination they appeared almost simultaneously at Cubberley High School. It was like viewing a mutation. All of a sudden a typical high school, with its football games and "senior prank day," found itself infected by a group of politically motivated students. If any of these kids had appeared alone, they would have been overlooked or ostracized. When sixty or so materialized and found each other, they accelerated their concerns about what they called a toxic society. They forced everyone around them to reevaluate what life was for, and how to use one's life for the benefit of humankind. Their presence totally altered the life of the school and the community around it.

I'll never forget seeing Mike and some other high school students working their politics in a demonstration at the Stanford Research Institute. The Stanford students and faculty of the Institute were mingling around the front of the building, discussing evidence that the Institute had been a CIA front—in fact, being used to train Asian and South American military police in surveillance and torture. They were debating the prospect of sitting in at the Institute and the need to avoid harm to any documents or research papers when Mike and several kids came on the scene. Mike immediately started to address the crowd. He admonished them for being surprised. "You claim to be objective scientists, but who determines what it is you study—who pays the bill? What happens to your work? You're not scientists, you're paid agents of the government."

As Mike was talking, the other high school students methodically stripped the building of its documents, presses, and other useful equipment. Mike was talking about the need for responsible action at the front of the building while his comrades were pulling shit like crazy out the back. When Mike finished, the audience of intelligentsia returned to its discourse about conducting a proper sit-in. "Be sure not to remove anything. It's important not to disturb any ongoing research. After all," it was argued, "years of professional lives are tied up in this place."

These high school revolutionaries were not polite. They acted to change a condition, not to preserve it. That's the fundamental difference between those who talk about change and those who take the risk and responsibility to do something.

The dream for a better society presented by these

young turks was a demanding cause. It required giving full life to your ideas about freedom and justice. There was no place for compromise. It was a challenge that most other students, parents, and faculty found too difficult to live with. Without any experience in making real decisions or working in a cooperative instead of a competitive way, the majority stumbled into an antagonistic position. It was simply easier to kill the dreamer than to live the dream. But wait, I'm getting ahead of my story.

When I first encountered these kids I felt confident that the American political system had the capacity to bring social justice. I believed that people were basically good. They didn't need a king or henchman to bring social order, but could rely on some kind of social contract between the governed and elected leaders. That if the governors got out of line they could always be recalled by public clamor. As for the schools' role in this scheme of things, well, they were to provide the young with experience in making decisions. Experience in collecting and measuring evidence about the way of life. Experience in building a better society. Learning the rights and responsibility of citizen kings. It was with this perspective that I eagerly looked forward to the practice of a student political club. I didn't have to wait long.

The Vietnam War crashed into American life like a brick through a window. As officers of Junior Statesmen, Doug, Sue, and Mike started bringing speakers to campus. They invited generals, scholars, and antiwar activists. Every Friday the Junior Statesmen sponsored a debate or lecture during the lunch hour. These meetings became the focal point of the school's attention. Each Friday hundreds of students crowded into tight classrooms to hear the arguments for and against the war. Gradually this forum became a Junior Statesmen platform solely dedicated to finding out why the war started, and how to stop it.

Junior Statesmen was a statewide organization sponsored by lawyers to instill in youth the mechanics of law
and debate as a prelude to enjoying the class benefit of some
day being a lawyer or legislator. Junior Statesmen selected
students for their intelligence and aptitude for leadership.
These students were then given extensive training in debate
skills and legal rights. The training culminated in having
the students actually sit in the chair of a legislator for a day
and conduct a mock senate. The students at Cubberley's
branch of Junior Statesmen used this experience not to
form the expected debate society or run student government; they acted to give their fellow students some control
over what was being presented in the schools as learning.
They questioned why schools are surrounded by chain-link
fences, why no student was allowed to participate in faculty
meetings. They requested a voice in setting curriculum and
determining the code of conduct for student behavior. And
most important of all, they demanded that the school take
up the questions of racism and Vietnam as they were mani-
fested in Palo Alto. Most of the argument for these rights
started with the school principal.

The principal was a young "Clark Kent"-looking
man. At twenty-nine he was probably the youngest principal in California secondary schools. Like the succession of
principals that came before him, he was on his way up. He
would be principal for a year or so in the prestigious Palo
Alto schools. Then he would move on to become superintendent in someplace like Illinois or Florida. He prided himself on being a card player—a poker player. He always sat
behind his desk as if he were in some kind of card game. It
was therefore difficult to know the man or his cause. Motionless. Always waiting for the next card. Or holding back
a smile, knowing he had an ace within reach. Like most
gamblers, his life centered on the fall of a card or the dealer's

choice. He had control of neither. Not knowing what the principal wanted or believed, I followed my own instincts and thoughts about political behavior for students and their advisor. And so the game began.

The students would invite a speaker onto campus. The principal would request a "pre-understanding" of what the speaker would say. The students would present the principal with an antiwar speech. Any antiwar speech would do. The principal would stipulate that the speakers use the small debate room so as not to interfere with students eating lunch or studying in the open courts. The students would overflow the assigned room and flow out into the court areas. The principal would deny the use of microphones or sound equipment, contending that these were only for sporting events. The students would bring their own loudspeaker system. The principal would demand the presentation of "the other side." The students would say fine—you present it. The principal required a mandatory presentation of the other side. The students dug huge bomb craters in the football field and ignited ash cans with jelly gasoline. That's the other side, they said. The principal banned the Junior Statesmen from campus.

Six hundred students and parents filled the School Board meeting called to decide the future of student political clubs. The School Board was comprised of local industrialists, realtors, and professionals. The leading industry in the town, Hewlett-Packard, had its board man in the form of Bernard Oliver. Bernard was jowled eloquence. Kind of a cross between William Buckley and Orson Welles. He waxed paternal control over every board meeting. He was the man. In arrogant undertone, he slighted everyone who came before him. His greatest sign of character was a slight upturn of the mouth whenever he would conclude a word duel with someone who was a little unsure or self-conscious. Mr. Oliver always had the last word. Usually he said something like, "When you have reached my age and experience, then you can tell the world what to do. Until then, it's best that you hide your ignorance by keeping silent." Upon hearing this, the inexperienced pundit would shrink in humility. In the shit-filled seconds that followed, Bernard's mouth would slowly curl into a malignant half-smile. Once again he had bested some thirteen-year-old, intimidated a teacher, or frightened a superintendent. Mr. Bernard Oliver was a big-timer.

Sitting on the board at the other end of the table was Mrs. Agnes Robinson. Now, she always smiled—a broad, toothy smile accompanied by a nodding head. Her appearance reminded one of a young Rose Kennedy. She was a good-hearted woman. Upon hearing any argument, she would take a little from each of the views and assemble them into a universal proposal to please everyone. She felt that any question could have a pleasant solution if only the protagonists would meet to talk out their differences. "A little give and take never hurt anyone . . ." was her reminder to the audience as the discussion of the banning of Junior Statesmen began.

Sue presented the case for allowing Junior Statesmen to remain active. She confidently announced to the crowded chamber, "It's our feeling that students have the right to bring political issues into the high school. To present speakers, political dramas, and films. This right stems from our desperate need to study and act on issues that directly affect our life. This right cannot be withdrawn by a school policy or even a state law because it is guaranteed in the Constitution of the United States. The right to freedom of expression. The right to assemble."

The audience remained still as she closed her remarks. It was hard being told by a young person what school policy should be. Even harder when that student was openly hostile to what most considered a "just war."

Mr. Oliver, sensing the restraint of the assembly, was quick to present his opinion on student activism. "First of all," he said, "you must understand that children in school just don't have all the rights afforded to adults. For example, a child can't be prosecuted in the same manner as an adult. And he can't take on financial liabilities. He can't even vote. A child in school just does not have the right to do as he pleases." Mr. Oliver turned his head, recognizing the rest of the board, and then continued. "And the idea that you have a club actively presenting a political position— why, that's absurd. Would you wish the Ku Klux Klan to have a club at your school? No, of course not."

The audience was in total agreement. Heads were waving support and a sprinkle of applause greeted Mr. Oliver's argument. Given this encouragement, he raised his voice to finish the issue. Looking straight at Sue, he cajoled and scolded with the same words. "I think it's marvelous that these young people show such an avid interest in politics. But I must strongly conclude that this interest belongs in the classroom." He excused Sue with a nod and called for the next agenda item.

Doug Monica slowly approached the board, then stopped, standing right alongside Sue and directly in front of Oliver. Oliver looked surprised, then perturbed. "Yes," he said anxiously, "is there something else?"

"Junior Statesmen is not comparable to the Ku Klux Klan because we have an open membership. And the politics you ask us to study in the classroom—it doesn't exist. Here is a copy of my civics book." Doug placed the large green book on the table in front of Mr. Oliver, then, turning and facing the audience, said, "There is no mention of the

Ku Klux Klan or racism, or labor struggles, or the Vietnam War. Not one word about honesty, or integrity, or even justice." Mr. Oliver looked uncomfortable. Doug continued with a stronger inflection. "How can we study politics if its forces and issues are missing from our books and classrooms?"

The assembly was still. Mr. Oliver gave a nervous laugh and shook his head, as if to say, "You crazy kids." Sue joined the questioning. "When do we become citizens?" she asked. "How do we learn to ask the right questions, take responsibility for our actions? When does this happen? Must we wait until we are in the military or working for you at Hewlett-Packard?" Mr. Oliver looked angry and started hammering his gavel to silence Sue's questions. She continued over the banging. "Is that the place where we are given the chance to speak, or will we be shut up there, too?"

Mr. Oliver erupted. "That's enough!" He moved to the edge of his chair and, leaning out to almost touch Doug and Sue, pointed his finger at them as if to shoot them. His words were fast and strong. "There is no place in school for students to form political clubs for the purpose of supporting Communist efforts in Vietnam or anywhere else in the world. I simply will not allow it." Mike Fox broke the assembly into laughter with a call from the back of the room. "The word Communist is also missing from our textbooks!" Confusion reigned. For the first time, Mr. Oliver had lost control of the board and the audience.

With sentences getting shorter and tension quickening, Mrs. Robinson entered the argument. "I think it's unfortunate that we can't come to some mutual understanding. I suggest that the board convene in a work session to construct a policy that encourages students to act as individuals, yet restricts the role of student clubs in advocating partisan politics." Mrs. Robinson's statement pulled the meeting out of its death grip. It was an appreciated respite. Sentiment had swung crazily throughout the meeting. Time was needed to absorb what had happened. In the calm, Doug turned to Mrs. Robinson and asked if students would work on this policy. Mrs. Robinson said yes. Whispers of applause greeted her response. The discussion of student clubs was temporarily over. Mr. Oliver had a small smile on his relaxing face.

The next day the superintendent informed the principal, who in turn informed me, that the Junior Statesmen club was to be disbanded immediately. I told the students of this decision. They greeted it with a surprise of their own. They voted to form a new club. The USM—United Student Movement. They asked me if I would be faculty advisor. I said yes. The principal asked me to take on some other assignments. I told him no. The principal informed me that I didn't understand the board's intention. I told him that he was right.

I had believed without question that people were basically good and capable of charting their own political destiny. After all, that's the fundamental premise behind the Constitution. That people have rights. To speak, assemble, and crusade. That mechanics exist in the vote, the referendum, the initiative to popularly direct a nation. That's what I learned as a student. And taught as a teacher. I didn't believe in the beauty of this "social contract," but I admired it. Wanted to practice it and make it work.

The student conflict with the school over the fundamental rights to speak and assemble gave me a sickening glimpse at the reality of this dream. The school and the institutions around it didn't encourage voices of protest, but insisted on cutting out their tongues. I began to feel that every word and thought being whispered by the students might be their last. Every meeting might be the last meeting. So I listened and strained to understand all that was being said. The thoughts were not pleasant. There was no "social contract" between student and school, just as there was no contract between consumer and Standard Oil, or soldier and the military, or citizen and the local unemployment office. They were not privy to the "corporate board meetings" that set the policies of their life. No, these constituents didn't have an elected official to vote out of office. In fact, they didn't have the vote. There was no mechanism for popular control of these institutions. No consensus, as Doug would say. The game was rigged. Not just for a few, but for almost everyone.

As a civics teacher I was amazed at what I didn't know or practice. Students claimed that police were hassling and arresting without cause any gathering of students who were downtown after eight o'clock. I didn't know if this was true and didn't know how to research the matter or publicly study it. Students claimed that several corporations in the Palo Alto area were making illegal fragment bombs. Again, I had no experience or idea about how to investigate this charge. Every day vital questions were being asked for which I as a teacher didn't have an answer, or even a procedure to supply an answer. Questions of corporate control over food prices and foreign policy seemed essential in the study of civics, yet the curriculum specified an emphasis on single and bicameral legislature. The history and civics I was teaching was obsolete, if not dangerous, in its avoidance of real issues and events. I didn't have a single tool or educational experience related to issues in land ownership, housing, pollution, hiring policies, police practice, health, or food, let alone the manifestations of these conditions into racial and violent morals. I was ashamed and alarmed at my ignorance.

Perhaps the most repelling thought was the growing reality that student questions were close to ugly realities. That somehow the practice of a nation guiding itself through popular controls was being replaced by silent governments in corporate buildings. That every aspect of life, from the bread you eat to the house you live in, to the energy you use, to the news you see, is made by individuals outside your control. That no matter how loud you yelled you could exercise no control over your life. It was like waking from a dream to find citizen kings replaced by a new set of unknown leaders called Exxon, Tenneco, and McDonald's. I didn't like it. I felt tricked and used.

Of course the real question is what to do. Do you throw yourself physically in the path of this waste machine, hoping to stall its progress or make it repent? Or practice civil disobedience? Refusing to pay its taxes and support its causes by accepting its recrimination of jail. Or do you close within yourself, trying to be a better individual and thereby hoping to inspire the rest of society with your humanitarian qualities? Or pick up the gun and assault the system with its own madness? Or build a commune in some remote place, hopefully outside the path of the slug called progress? Or is there nothing to do except indulge in a last orgy—watch the butterflies die, the seeds drop on still ground? What do you do?

The meeting to decide that very thing was at hand. My mind knew things that my heart wouldn't accept.

Like the nation, I was without vision. Events seemed to dictate action more than reason. Life at school felt like being the shiny ball inside a pinball machine. The players in this life-and-death drama were pushed and hurried in every direction. Lights rang up in the form of headlines, but all one felt was the relentless pounding. Body counts of war dead. Casualties. The number of protesters at each demonstration rang in the news, telling a toll. No one knew who was winning. The noise and lights obliterated everything. The only certainty was that you couldn't escape. The score climbed into the hundreds and then thousands . . . and the game continued.

The school refused students the right to pass out anti-war literature. The students wrote their message in chalk on the school pavement. School officials used the school intercom to warn of suspensions for anyone marking school property. The students printed their message on napkins and filled the cafeteria with disposable propaganda. School officials confiscated the napkins and warned of arrest for anyone distributing leaflets. Students painted words of protest on their faces. They were arrested. Flowers planted by students in the winter began to break the earth in front of the school in the form of a peace symbol. They were dug up.

A School Board meeting was called. It was the fifth of its kind to discuss student activism. The United Student Movement and any other student political club was banned from campus. Any student participating in such a club would be permanently expelled.

And so here we are. The last meeting of the USM. It's time to decide what to do next. I've been day-dreaming through the meeting. Looking at these children as if this might be my last chance. Reviewing in my mind the gestures and events that marked their brilliance. Those moments when just for a second they had the pained expression or exuberance of a child. Their masks were hardening daily. Soon you would see nothing but the faces of revolution. And I've been thinking about myself—how much I've changed. The bitter disappointments in not being able to involve the faculty in this student movement. Of being so alone. And afraid. Questioning where all this madness would end.

Doug was concluding the discussion. The step was taken. It was decided to take the protest against the war into the streets. To march against the Oakland Induction Center. And if possible disrupt its operation. To block the streets with people. Halt the buses carrying draftees. Hold the war still for as long as possible. Resist any attempt by police to move the people or the buses. Fight with rocks.

Sue provided the last pieces of advice "to protect your balls, stuff gym socks into your underwear. Right here, up front, where it will do the most good. Vaseline applied to the face is also a good idea. If you feel the sting of gas, don't rub at it. Keep your hands away from your eyes. There will be cold water at the first aid station. This is your bail number. Write it on your arm or the back of your hand. It's important not to carry any weapons. We don't want to get someone hurt. Stay together. Watch for each other and help anyone that gets jammed. . . ."

Her words were greeted with silence. There was no hurrah or sense of gallantry. No romantics. It was a sad occasion. A detachment or uncoupling with school was taking place. Familiar things were being set aside for the unknown. In this awkward moment Doug turned to me and asked if I had anything to say. We both knew my words would not alter events or provide enlightenment. It was a funny gesture. Perhaps it was Doug's way of saying thank you for sticking it out. Or was he, like the others in the room, looking back for one more opportunity to sense the school as a protected place to argue ideas and fight for what's right? I don't know.

It was a strange sensation that held me at this moment. I felt like a participant in some unpracticed ritual of goodbye. I didn't know what to do. Should I behave like a Japanese emperor and wish them all an honorable journey, or scold them for their impatience and brashness? No, they

knew full well what sacrifice they were making. And so did
I. They were taking a step that I knew I couldn't take. My
mind raced for a second on that thought. Why are we parting and why can't I simply go with them? Fight with all my
worth for an end to the war and the practice of greed and
exploitation that caused it. Take up the rock and whatever
follows. There can be no compromise with this war. Surely
I must act. If my mouth is gagged, then I must kick with my
arms and legs. Anything less is cowardice. As I invited these
thoughts I felt the full impact of cultural blocks falling and
sliding into place. Like the sealing of an Egyptian tomb, the
stones were closing any prospect of joining such a renegade
act. Fear of being alone was there. Of being hurt. And causing pain to those I love. I rationalized about being trained to
repeat information, not to collect or act on information.
But even stronger was the cultural block against abusing
property and the absolute prohibition against taking life.
These were hurdles that I couldn't step over. Where they
came from and why they were so strong I can only guess. I
simply couldn't escape my past.

My own working-class background was in the way.
Wearing clean underwear so that in event of an accident the
hospital attendants will know you come from a "good family." A good family that gives the future to benign gods, em-
ployers, and governmental leaders. How amusing. These
prep revolutionaries act for a class they know nothing
about. Maybe they can create a new class of socially conscious people. I wish them well in this struggle. I can only
wish.

Doug interrupted my thoughts with the question,
"Mr. Jones, what happens to USM?" It was like a student
asking a question. The old days. I had an answer. Students
sat waiting for a final lesson. Like a prerehearsed play, we
all engaged in this last discourse. It was something to do.

Something we knew how to do. A final classroom meeting of the United Student Movement. Complete with teacher, students, and curriculum.

It's not as if I didn't really know this moment would come. I expected and even prepared for it. I had learned a great deal about myself during the past months from these children mentors and their cause. Countless times I was forced to make decisions that defined a personal political character. For my own survival I had carefully delineated what I believed and what it was I must do when faced with the question of violent political protest. Now it was time to teach what I had learned.

I walked to the front of the room and stood facing the class. This was the first time I had ever addressed the club in this manner. It felt strange, this last play of roles. A final showing of respect.

I started my lecture with an announcement. "I withdraw my faculty sponsorship of the USM," then explained my reason for this decision. It was obvious that the student voice and organizing effort was going off campus and into the community. It was also apparent that student-initiated efforts against the war would not be limited to the use of speech, but indeed would move to forms of direct confrontation with the institutions that supported the war. And so I argued, "You will no longer be acting within the law or even in a civil disobedient manner. You have chosen to work outside the law. The act of revolution that you contemplate is an extremely personal decision. I don't want that decision clouded by membership in a club. If you decide to act tomorrow, you do so on your own."

Following this announcement, I set about tracing the political journey traveled by the USM. Its early requests for the constitutional rights to speak and assemble. The use of petitions, meetings with school officials, and legal suits.

The use of civil disobedience to protest unjust and improper restrictions on these rights. The peaceful sit-ins and class boycotts. The acceptance of arrest as necessary for peaceful protest. And finally the decision to move outside established channels and civil disobedient forms of protest into civil warfare. In a matter of months the full gamut of political action had been deeply experienced. In academic terms I described the boundaries that had been crossed. The realities that lay ahead. Like most lectures, it contained the facts but somehow missed the motives and desires that drive human conduct. The lecture ended. I simply ran out of words.

The USM was finally over. I would no longer have to suffer the hate-filled stare of faculty members or intimidation from the school superintendent. No longer would I have to argue long hours about politics. Or drive kids home from jail because they dared to speak their cause. It was like a shedding of a great coat. I felt lighter and free.

Doug and the other students were beginning to leave. They filed past, saying goodbye and thanks, some wishing me good luck. Promises to come back and talk with the sophomore classes. We were parting friends. Finally Doug passed. After all these weeks we had never quite been able to trust each other. He shrugged and told me not to let the faculty put me down. Sue followed Doug. She grabbed my hand and held it while Doug talked. She didn't say a word. Mike, as usual, was last to leave the room. I had tried to recruit him for the basketball team and in the process we became good friends. He, of all the students in the USM, maintained a rare sense of humor. He put his arm around me and, like a coach addressing a player, said with a broad smile, "See ya, Mr. Jones, tomorrow in Oakland."

The next morning a Cubberley High School history teacher took part in a demonstration at the Oakland Induction Center. I was that teacher. I couldn't escape the future.

We Killed Them

Friday, June 19, 8:30 A.M.

"We're gonna kill them bums, Mr. Jones. Kill 'em. That's right. You'll see. Right, Mr. Jones? We're gonna kill them!" Michael Rice is sliding into his cushioned airline seat, jabbing words at me through a confident smile: "You'll see. We're gonna murder them guys!" My eyes follow Michael into his seat and watch Eddie Cotter help him with the safety belt. I count to myself. Michael and Eddie in the seats in front of me, Joey next to me, and Audie and Jimmy across the aisle. Good. Everyone's here. I count one more time. All five are on the plane. In the past hour I have mentally lassoed these five a dozen times. In the next two days, I will count to five perhaps a thousand times. Together, we make up the San Francisco Special Olympics Basketball Team. We're part of a large group of Olympians traveling to the state competition.

Michael twists in his seat so he can reach back and grab my hand. Just as I think he is going to change the topic of conversation, he smiles and reminds me of our mission. "Coach, we're gonna kill 'em."

Michael is the team's leader, mostly because of his size and generosity. When standing, Michael bends for-

ward like a top-heavy tree, and in motion he shuffles his feet
as if on a slippery surface. Like the other players, Michael
cannot add a row of numbers or write a sentence. He has
not learned about Racism, Republicanism, East or
Westism. The social baggage we carry is irrelevant to
Michael. Michael welcomes strangers into his thoughts by
throwing his arm around them and courting their interest
with a barrage of enthusiastic chatter. His thoughts are
disarmingly honest and to the point, even if they are
repetitious. And though his words are predictable, his enthusiasm and affection are always a wonderful surprise. So
I hold hands with this kindly giant who is talking of murder
and smiling of life. And I wait to be hugged by him at some
unexpected moment. I know I will find myself jumping ex-
citedly into the air with Michael over some soon-to-be accomplishment or commonplace event. I am stuck between
two worlds: my world of educated reason that tells me to
pay attention, and Michael's world of open enthusiasm and
affection that tells me I will perform miracles. His world
reminds me that the miracle is waiting in Los Angeles and it
will not be orchestrated by reason.

Michael's seatmate, Eddie Cotter, doesn't like the
idea of Michael's standing. Eddie points all around the
cabin, showing Michael that everyone is seated. Then he
tells everyone about seat belts. "Put on your seat belt. Like
this! Here, Michael Rice, put on your seat belt like this."

Eddie is the team's lawyer. He worries constantly
about what is "right" and the performance of "rightness."
"Isn't that right, Mr. Jones? It's time. Come on, you guys.
It's time to put on your seat belts. Joey, you put on your seat
belt like this. This is the way you do it." Joey will have none
of it. He is listening to Michael's jabber about mayhem on
the court. And every time Michael says the word "kill," Joey

yelps his approval and shakes both fists in the air. So I reach over and buckle Joey's seat belt.

In between Michael's game plan and Eddie's seat-belt plan, I ask Joey if this is his first time on an airplane. Joey nods yes, and punctuates the nod with a great gulp of air. Continuing our conversation, Joey throws a hand in the air, school-boy style, and slowly bends his fingers, until one finger points skyward.

"Yes," I answer, "we're number one. We can't miss with these killer black uniforms, now can we?" I know my words will make Joey smile. He can't hide his feelings or form words, so he "talks" by flooding you with his emotions. And it works. His smile and raspy sounds are telepathic. At the mention of our uniforms, Joey's eyes light up. He tilts his head back and lets loose with a choking laugh. Then, with his eyes still glistening, he directs a question at me. He points at his uniform bag, then rubs my shirt.

"No," I respond, "I don't have a uniform. I'm the coach—remember?"

Joey grins in acknowledgement. Eddie continues talking about seat belts. Michael talks on about winning. Joey uses his clenched handkerchief to catch saliva rolling from his open mouth. I count to five.

Other passengers are now boarding the plane. They look stunned at row after row of athletes wearing bright yellow hats, blue warm-up jerseys, and disabled bodies. The Olympians snap their stares by applauding them. A ripple of clapping greets each passenger as he filters toward the rear of the plane. These travelers are not expecting applause; they smile nervously as the many Olympians reach out to touch them or wave hello. Within moments, athletes and passengers are shaking hands, exchanging sign language, and sharing destinations.

"Where are you kids going?"

"To Los Angeles!"

"Who are you, I mean, who do you represent, all dressed up like this?"

"We're going to Los Angeles!"

"What's going to go on down there?"

"We're gonna kill them!"

"Oh. Good luck."

"You too!"

The stewardess is reading the mandatory emergency procedures. Each precaution is met by wild cheers. Methodically, every yellow hat turns upward to find the invisible oxygen mask, and looks to the rear of the cabin for the emergency door, and under the seat for the mysterious flotation cushion.

Then the attention of the Olympians turns to the sensation of movement. The plane is beginning to tiptoe. Great applause from the yellowcappers. We are on our way to Los Angeles. Like some winged horse, the plane glides down the runway, and with a final push sails cloudward. More applause. And yelling. This time, *all* the passengers are clapping.

I count heads. Michael and Eddie. Joey. Audie and Jimmy. Audie grabs my counting finger. His eyes are wide with fear. "I'm going to fall! I'm too high!"

"Audie," I say, "it's all right. It's all right. Audie, the plane has wings—see, out there. Those are wings and the air 'lifts'. . . um, the motors push the plane . . . we're riding on waves of air created by—Audie, look at me. Audie, if you fall, I promise to catch you!" My explanation of air travel doesn't exactly calm Audie's fear. It doesn't exactly instill me with confidence either. Fortunately for both of us, the stewardess arrives with the Coca-Cola cure.

Audie enjoys his Coke. He taps my hand and asks, "Bathroommm. Bathroommm." I point to the line at the front of the plane as if something important is about to happen.

Audie is perhaps the strongest and fastest athlete in this contingent. As a basketball player, however, he has trouble with direction. When he rebounds, he returns the ball to the closest basket. About half the time his shots are aimed at what Eddie calls the "right" basket. The rest of the time, he is a fantastic scoring threat for the other team. Any basket sets off a spasm of delight—pure joy that is hard to stifle with the message that, "Audie, you have just scored two points for the other team!"

Audie lives in high gear. Nothing he does is slow or deliberate. I guess that's why I selected Audie for our basketball team. When he shoots down the floor like a grinning rocket, I can point to the ball he leaves behind. I hope basketball will help Audie get a little control. Slow down. Run in the right direction. Well, he's going in the right direction this time—to the front of the plane—and that's an accomplishment.

I do a quick body count. Michael has his arm around Eddie, talking about the right uniform to wear. Joey is gulping his Coke. Audie is in line. Jimmy Powers, his seatmate, is asleep. It's 8:50.

Friday, 7:00 P.M.

We are in a sea of color. Three thousand athletes from all over California are assembled at Drake Field on the UCLA campus for the opening ceremony of the Special Olympics. Jimmy is the shortest player on our team, so I hold his hand as waves of athletic teams move about us. Joey holds my other hand. Michael, Eddie, and Audie walk ahead of us, arm-in-arm, like the Three Musketeers. Pride and friendship are on parade. Just as we hold each other, the sky and earth seem to move closer—brushing softly against the banners, listening to the muffled sounds of excitement and peals of laughter, joining us in this celebration.

Michael is the first to let the air out of Camelot. "Those suckers are big! Mr. Jones, do you SEE those suckers? Oh, brother, those suckers are BIG!" Sure enough, Michael is right. I stop dreaming and start being a coach. I count several towering figures wearing the red warm-ups of Fresno. And there's a giant wearing the orange and white of Tri-Valley. Michael Rice is our tallest player at six feet, four inches. These guys look closer to seven feet. "Mr. Jones, see that tall dude over there? Those suckers are mean."

I begin to question myself. I mean, asking Joey to play on our team was unavoidable. I know that you're not supposed to have favorites in teaching, but Joey and I are best friends. We liked each other immediately. I think he liked the fact I played sports, and I loved Joey for the way he played sports. Joey moves like a mechanical soldier. His arms are stuck in a bent position and his gait is an awkward side-to-side gallop—a gallop that races full tilt, unable to change direction or stop. To slow down, Joey often runs into things or throws his body on the ground. I guess it's that will to charge ahead, full speed, knowing he can't stop, that I admire. He has more spirit than an evangelist on a hot summer night, but he can't even catch a ball, much less dribble or shoot.

And Jimmy. Little Jimmy. He can dribble and shoot if no one stands in front of him. It's going to take more than Joey's spirit to help Jimmy even see the ball. I wish Jimmy were two feet taller. And Audie a lot slower. And Eddie

—well, Eddie might be able to get the ball to Michael if he can stop debating with himself about what's the right thing to do.

It's time to start some reality therapy.

"You know, you guys, I've got an idea." Michael, Eddie, Joey, Audie, and Jimmy glue themselves to my side. "I was thinking, we need a team motto—you know, something special that we can share, like a secret." The conspiracy thickens as my thoughts are welded by a uniform "ALL RIGHT!" "Good, our secret pledge for these games is *togetherness*," "YEAH!" I lower my voice, "And instead of shouting all over the place that we're number one, I think it's better that we become number five." I put up five fingers and give each finger a player's name. "In this tournament, let's not worry so much about number one. Our job is for each player to go as hard as he can. Instead of saying we're number one, let's say we're number five."

I stretch all five fingers in the air and hear a roar from my cohorts. "We're number five! We're number five!" This attempt at humility is followed by an unprompted, "We're gonna kill them! You watch." Eddie tailors his words. "We'll win, right? You'll see, Mr. Jones. We'll win those big guys."

Everyone agrees with Eddie. "We're gonna murder them," Michael adds. "We'll clobber them big suckers. We're number one!" The whole team shouts with Michael, "We're number one!" Joey smiles; Eddie shakes his head in the affirmative; Audie jumps up and down; Jimmy holds both small fists in mid-air; Michael holds up one finger—which is greeted by a unanimous, "We're number one!"

I look around and every team in my circle of vision chants a similar claim. The big players from Fresno and Tri-Valley have their arms in the air. I fantasize that they can dunk the ball without jumping. Everyone around us is yelling, "We're number one! We're Number One!" I join the chorus and close Camelot's drawbridge on thoughts of x's and o's and tall centers.

We're Number One.

We're Number One.

I hope.

Saturday, 5:30 A.M.

I'm right in the technicolor part of a great dream. Good outlet pass. Fill the lanes. Here comes Audie. Pull up. Float a pass rim-high. Audie slams it through. Joey and I are playing the tough defense. We double-team the ball. Joey tips it free. I'm after it. So who's knocking? What has that got to do with defense? A seven-foot center skittles in my way. The door is being pounded like a drum. Bang—Bang—Bang. Thoughts of fire drill, aerial bombardment, and a loose ball race around in my head. Bang—Bang—Bang. I place a hand over my eye sockets to end the mental filmworks. And slowly, very slowly, find the barking door. When I open it, I am assaulted by a blast of cold fluorescent light. And something else. At first I can't quite make out who or what is standing in the hallway. Moving figures look like members of some assassin cult come to get me in the middle of the basketball game. They're talking about death. When my squint becomes an eye opening, I find myself staring at five basketball players in full armor. It is 5:30 in the morning and the entire basketball team is outside my door, dressed and ready to kill.

On closer examination I notice that these warriors are not all that ready. Michael has tied Joey's shoes, but Joey has to hold up his pants—actually he is pinching his arms against his hips. Audie's pants are on inside out. Jimmy is holding his supporter in one hand, asking where it goes.

Eddie is telling him. "It goes in your bag. Right, Mr. Jones? It goes in your bag."

I shake off a dozen questions and ask one of my own. "Are you guys going to breakfast in your uniforms?" It's a silly question. Of course we go to breakfast in our uniforms. White jersey tops with black numerals, black silk shorts trimmed in white, Converse All-Stars, and white high-top socks with three black rings. When I ask Michael why everyone got into white tops instead of black, he answers matter of factly, "We're saving the black tops for the championship game."

Game One, Saturday, 10:00 A.M.

Our warm-up consists of everyone getting a free shot. Every careen of the ball prompts applause and excited yells of triumph. Joey and Audie have to race for the bathroom or risk peeing in their new uniforms. Michael rebounds each shot with a thud. Eddie paces. Joey returns to give encouragement. With each shot, he waves his crooked arms in the air like an official signaling a touchdown. When someone makes a basket, or comes close, Joey violently throws his arms down and let's out a guttural sound of pleasure. Michael pounds the loose ball and announces, "This is it, Mr. Jones. This is the moment we've been waiting for. This is it!" Joey roars agreement. Audie runs around in a circle under the basket, with both hands in the air, yelling, "Now. Now. Now!"

The first game is against Tri-Valley. It's scheduled to last ten minutes, and then the team with the most points will be declared the winner. The purpose of the game is to place teams into divisions of equal ability. The score at the end of ten minutes is 16 to 2. We get the last two points when Michael sinks a twenty-foot running hook, our only basket. Nobody seems to care. Michael roars off the court and picks up Joey. Eddie congratulates Michael and asks what the score is now. Audie is still running down the court, unaware that the game is over. Jimmy takes a Muhammad Ali victory pose and asks if he did okay. I answer, "Man, you did, everyone did great. Just great! I was proud of you. That shot of Michael's was superb. I think if we work a little more on our defense we'll. . . ." Michael finishes the sentence—"We'll kill them!"

Actually I'm worried. We've been blown away sixteen to two. That places us in the lowest ability division, but even that is hard to take for someone who hates to lose. I can't help my feelings. For too many years I have played and coached basketball. Something happens when I get inside a gym. I love it. Love to play and love to win. Every intuitive and intellectual antenna clicks into automatic at the sight of another team doing lay-ups. I find myself scouting our opponents, scrutinizing the line-up of teams, pushing my team on the floor to practice at every available free time. It's that extra effort, that extra lap or free throw that will make the difference. That's what I think while I have everyone take defensive positions and attack the movement of the ball. We practice holding our hands up, cutting off the baseline, stopping the dribbler. If we play defense, we just might have a chance. Defense is something you can teach. Offense is an art.

Game Two, Saturday, 2:00 P.M.

We draw Southeast Los Angeles. You can tell the course of a game in the first few seconds. The Los Angeles team executes a tip-off play, streaks the length of the floor, and scores the first two points. Then steals the inbounds pass for a quick four-point lead. Michael tries to take command of the game. He dribbles the length of the floor and casts off from the top of the key. The ball banks off the backboard and into a fast break. The score is six to nothing. I yell at Michael, "Get underneath, let Eddie handle the ball, get underneath!" Jimmy gets the ball. He tries to advance the ball up the court, but is surrounded by a wall of red uniforms. The ball kicks loose and a Los Angeles player sinks a jump shot. "My God. Did you see that shot—that kid could play for the Lakers!" I call time out.

In the huddle, I explain what I think is our only hope. "Look, Eddie, you dribble the ball up the court and feed the ball in deep to Michael—you got that? Michael, you take the ball and go right up with it. . . . okay, Michael? This is the time—go for your sky hook!"

The team explodes back onto the floor loaded with confidence and visions of Michael's sky hook. I sit down, then stand back up. Michael is dribbling the length of the floor. "No, Michael, no. Get in the key!" It's a set shot from thirty feet. The ball hits nothing. . . but net. "Two, two, yahoo! What a shot! Nice going, Jimmy. Now we're going. Come on, you guys, defense. Get back. Get back. Oh, no." Following our basket, the entire team races to congratulate Jimmy. The other team throws a court-length pass for a lay-up.

During this seesaw war, Michael never does get in the pivot. I point. Jump up and down. Even run along the sidelines screaming instructions. "Michael, get under the basket. No, no, no. Don't dribble the ball." They have another steal, and another. It is Xerox time. "Michael, let Eddie bring up the ball; get underneath. Michael—down there, get down there where you belong. . . ." The five in white run around officials and past the bench and to the key, and back across the center line to the other end. Drop the ball. Kick it. Roll over it. Only to do it all over again.

We lose 58 to 6. The score doesn't bother me as much as what this humiliation might mean for my killers in white. Michael played like a lion. He sensed the onslaught and tried all by himself to balance the score. No one could have tried harder. Eddie was simply unable to calculate the right place to be or the right pass to make. You could feel his hesitation as he rocked his arms, looking for someone to pass to or some place to run toward. Joey valiantly chased the ball the entire game. No matter where the ball went, Joey was in pursuit. Throughout the game, he didn't touch the ball. Not once. Several times he galloped right past a loose ball, grinning all the way, his arms waving like iron gates. Audie circled during most of the game, with both hands raised above his head, signaling for someone, any-one, anytime, to throw him a pass. Jimmy tried and tried and tried. I am afraid the team's heart will be broken.

The tournament official comes up to me and stuffs a large brown envelope into my hand. "Here," he says in a soft voice. "Here are the participation medals for your team— your guys might need a little pickup." Together we crank our heads to see how my team is taking their loss. What we see hits us with a jolt. Michael has led everyone over to the roll of mats at the end of the next court. The team is kneel-ing on the mats, cheering for a game in progress. Whooping it up for baskets made and passes completed. And in the midst of their yells, we both hear a spirited challenge— "We're gonna kill you guys!"

The official hangs on to his envelope. "Maybe you don't need this. I mean, where did your team get its spirit? They might be the worst team in the tournament and here they are challenging everyone in sight to a shoot-out at high noon." My shrug doesn't answer his question, so he con-tinues. "Do they know they just lost?"

I offer an idea. "I don't think they know the difference between winning and losing!" We are both shaking our heads in admiration and disbelief.

The official takes back his envelope. "Well, coach, you've got one more chance to get a medal. If you can win this afternoon at four against Sonoma, well then you can play tomorrow for a third place medal in your division. Who knows, those characters might yell themselves a medal."

I walk slowly over to my team. They are bubbling with enthusiasm, pointing to good plays and shouting familiar directions. "Get back, get back, you turkeys. Hands up! Hands up!" They seem wired to the play. Every nuance and gesture is picked up. A player's happiness and success is immediately known and shared by the observers. It's almost as if my team were playing another game. By throwing their voices onto the court, they participate in the game.

I have always seen the game as a match-up of strategies. If one team throws up a zone, you move the ball and overload one side of the court. If an opponent is superior in ability, you slow down the game tempo. If you get ahead late in the game, you spread your offense and force your opponent to play man-to-man defense. If behind, you double-team the ball and pressure the offense. . . . My team is watching another game and enjoying it as much as any game ever played.

I'm thinking that I want to know more about this other game when Joey jerks in front of me. He points across the floor—and then jabs his hand into his chest. I nod, yes, expecting Joey to romp for the bathroom. Joey runs straight into the game in progress. He simply joins in, chasing the ball around trying to vacuum it up with his mechanical arms. I jump after him. In between passes and fast breaks, I chase Joey around the court. When I catch him, we both join our team. They are cheering Joey and me. And the game in progress. And future games. And their own prowess. If an alien force were to ask me about the game of basketball, I don't know who I'd send forward. . . . Alvin Attles or Joey Asaro.

Saturday, 9:00 P.M.

We've made it to the big game—by accident. The Saturday afternoon game with Sonoma was a forfeit—their bus broke down. So we played against ourselves and won. Actually, several nieces, nephews, and parents joined me in playing our Olympic team. It was the most enjoyable basketball game I've ever played. The sidelines were like rubber bands. We chased, pushed, pulled each other. Ran with the ball, passed it, tripped over it, and hugged it. Kept our own score. Forgot the score. Made up a score. Took pleasure in all manner of accomplishment.

Our self-imposed win places us in Sunday's game for third place medals against a San Diego team. As far as our team is concerned, we have won and now we are about to play for the championship of the world.

Saturday night's waiting seems interminable. Five uniformed players hover about me like moths at a lamp. Every moment is filled with poking fingers, pumping hands, and landslides of conjecture. Eddie, weighing every possibility . . . over and over. "We should wear our black uniforms, right? We can wear them now, it's all right now, we can wear our black uniforms. Isn't it all right, Mr. Jones?" Sandwiched around Eddie's thoughts is Michael's insistence. "Too much for those guys. They don't stand a chance. Not against us. We're gonna annihilate those turkey legs from San Diego." Piercing into this constant din is Audie's fix: "What time is it? What time tomorrow? Do we play, what time in our black uniforms?" These three sentiments chase each other around and around. I feel I am being eaten alive by enthusiasm.

"Look, you guys have to calm down. The game isn't until twelve o'clock tomorrow." Like an endless string of firecrackers, the mention of the game simply kicks off another round of excitement. In desperation, I try hallway exercises. After an hour, I am beat. Audie wants to go to the bathroom and the remainder of the team keeps doing windmills, while jogging in place. Now in greater desperation, I try a late-night food raid. I figure if they eat something, anything, the talking cycle will be broken. Dressed in killer black uniforms, we attack the candy machines in the dormitory lobby. Evidently we are not the only team in training. The machines are overdosed on athletes plunking in odd assortments of coinage and then pushing all the buttons as fast as possible. The telephone in the lobby has been reduced to a sound that cries the end of the world. It isn't a dial tone or a busy signal but a steady whine. On this night before the BIG GAME, even God must be a little confused.

Announcing "lights out," I discover Joey kneeling, bent in prayer, crossing himself over and over. When he finishes, I ask softly, "What are you praying for?" Joey gyrates with his hands. My mind is answering for him—what a wonderful moment, he's saying the Lord's Prayer. The urgency of his gestures serves to question my assumption. His hand is in a fist that stirs the air. Then a finger straightens to point at me and the Converse shoes placed at the end of his bed. I offer, "Joey, you're praying for the basketball team." No, his head thunders. He hits towards me with clenched hands and lower lip curled into a grimace.

"You want to win tomorrow," I suggest. No, goes the head. Michael enters the room and joins my interpretations. He knows immediately what I don't want to see. Joey sweeps into motion. He crosses himself in a spastic fashion and then smiles and hits outward. Michael knows what Joey is praying for. "We're gonna kill them, right, Joey?" Joey grins in the affirmative, then, like the other players, crawls into sleep wearing a starchy black uniform.

Game Four, Sunday, Noon

So here we are, at last. This is it. The Big Game. The San Diego team is a little shorter than we are, but they have a pair of good shooters. And to get into this game, they've actually won a real game. Scored 26 points against Butte County. That 26 points scares me. On the basis of our warm-up shooting, I calculate it would take us three games to score that many baskets. And that's without a defense. I contemplate putting Michael and Eddie on the San Diego shooters and letting everyone else run around in a zone. No, it's not a time for match-ups, or strategy. It's a time to play hard and enjoy whatever happens. I decide to let Michael bring the ball down the court and give the team a simple rule: "If the ball comes to you, shoot!"

Both teams line up, not sure of which basket they defend or hope to shoot at. Michael gets the tip. The ball goes straight up and when it comes down, he is waiting for it. He dribbles straight ahead, full speed. Right for the basket. No one is in his way. When he stops to shoot, the trailing players pour by him. He is still alone. His shot rolls around the rim and falls off. Michael stretches his body and catches the ball with his arms extended. From this flat-footed stance, he pushes the ball once again at the target. This time it goes in. "Holy hot potato!" Pure exhilaration. The first two points are ours. "Get back! Get back!" Five players clad in black race backward. "That's it! That's it! Hands up!"

They form a straight line—one behind each other, like some picket fence. It's a new defense called stand-in-a-row. I am tempted for just a moment to yell instructions, to spread them out. No. "Hands up!" The fence grows a row of points that steal the pass. "Audie, this way. Audie, dribble the ball." Audie dribbles. He isn't running full tilt without the ball. Or circling. Or surrendering with his waving hands. Audie has his head down and he's dribbling. Dribbling under control past the half-court circle. "Keep going, Audie. Keep going."

Audie picks up the ball to run around several defensive players, but then puts it back on the floor in a controlled dribble. Within radar range of the right hoop, he jumps into the air and flings the ball toward the metal ring. The ball kisses the ring and almost skids in. Audie is jumping up and down. Joey is tracking the now-loose ball. In the rebound effort, it kicks loose and is bouncing toward our basket. Joey is right behind it. So is a San Diego player. The other player scoops up the ball and veers for a sure lay-up. It's too hard. Joey is now running the other direction full speed.

All the players on the floor are running after the San Diego lay-up attempt. Joey and the ball are flying past them, going the other direction. The two forces almost collide. Joey is now by himself chasing a ball that he has been pursuing for three games: "Go for it! Joey, get in front of it!" All the players realize that they have just overrun the ball and they begin to chase. At the three-quarter mark, Joey lunges at the moving ball. His momentum only serves to push the ball further beyond his reach. "Joey, slow down. Let it go out of bounds. Let it go."

Joey can't slow down. And doesn't want to try. He continues to run toward the wall at the end of the gym. I've seen that determination before. I start running after him. Then I see what Joey has in his mind. He dives for the ball. If he misses, he slams head first into a doorway. If he hits it, I don't—Joey lands on the ball. Its forward spin and shape punch Joey's body skyward. His arms wrap around the rubber like a child grappling with a favorite doll. He won't let go or be tossed off. The dive is followed by a bounce upward and a violent roll. Over and over, ball and Joey, Joey and the ball. They slam into the wall. Joey has his catch. He's got the ball. He jumps up in that awkward way he has. And holds the ball against his chest. His face is wide with pleasure. The official following the play doesn't know what to do. Everyone stops, surrounding Joey and the ball. They are both a good twenty feet outside the end line. Joey's smile indicates that something wonderful has happened. The official gives ceremony to this catch. He whistles loudly three times; then with great NBA flare, he yells, "Out of bounds. San Diego ball."

Joey grins and nods his head, and unconsciously hops on one leg. He releases the ball by pulling both arms aside. The ball drops into the official's waiting hand. Joey races to take his place in the picket-fence defense. I'm cheering inside. And crying. Yelling, "Defense. Come on." Joey shakes his fist in acknowledgment.

Somewhere in those first few moments of play, the floor tilts in our favor. It is one of those games where everything goes one way. Players get loose and then unstoppable. Michael, Eddie, Joey, Audie, and Jimmy become the players in their minds. They are Kareem and Dr. Dunk, Magic Johnson and a thousand television images. They fly down the floor. Tip the ball in. Throw court-length bombs. Make baskets only dreamed about.

Before I can turn around, Audie is jumping at me. I

catch his hips at eye level and absorb his crashing body. Joey
lands on both of us, pounding us with his handkerchief fist.
Michael catches the three of us in a great hug. Jimmy and
Eddie join our dance.

We've won—42 to 12.

Everyone on the floor is jumping up and down.
Shaking hands. Slapping backs. Even the San Diego players
seemed delighted by events. I search out the San Diego
coach. I want to apologize for not being able to keep the
game closer. In the blur of bodies, waving towels, and flying
uniform tops, I find the San Diego coach and express my
concern.

"I'm sorry, coach, I couldn't keep things a little more
in control." The San Diego coach smiles broadly and points
at his team. "Look, you kiddin'? My kids think they killed
you!"

Also available from Island Press, Star Route 1, Box 38, Covelo, California 95428

The Christmas Coat, by Ron Jones. Illustrations. $4.00
A contemporary fable of a mysterious Christmas gift and a father's search for the sender, which takes him to his wife, his son, and his memories of big band and ballroom days.

Wellspring: A Story from the Deep Country, by Barbara Dean. Illustrations. $6.00
A woman's life in tandem with nature—the honest, often beautiful telling of one woman's life in a rugged setting, both geographically and emotionally. "A life of gritty determination, monasticism and the pioneer spirit."—San Francisco *Examiner*

Headwaters: Tales of the Wilderness, by Ash, Russell, Doog, and Del Rio. Preface by Edward Abbey. Photographs and illustrations. $6.00
Four bridge-playing buddies tackle the wilderness—they go in separately, meet on top of a rock, and come out talking. These four are as different as the suits in their deck of cards, as ragged as a three-day beard, and as eager as sparks.

The Search for Goodbye-to-Rains, by Paul McHugh. $7.50
Steve Getane takes to the road in an American odyssey that is part fantasy and part real—a haphazard pursuit that includes Faulkner's Mississippi, the rarefied New Mexico air, and a motorcycle named Frank. "A rich, resonant novel of the interior world. Overtones of Whitman, Kerouac."—Robert Anton Wilson

An Everyday History of Somewhere, by Ray Raphael. Illustrations by Mark Livingston. Photographs. $8.00
These pages embrace the life and work of ordinary people, from the Indians who inhabited the coastal forests of northern California to the loggers, tanbark strippers, and farmers who came after them. This loving look at history takes us in a full circle that leads straight to the everyday life of us all.

The Book of the Vision Quest: Personal Transformation in the Wilderness, by Steven Foster with Meredith E. Little. Photographs. $10.00
The inspiring record of modern people enacting an ancient, archetypal rite of passage. This book shares the wisdom and the seeking of many persons who have known the opportunity to face themselves, their fears and their courage, and to live in harmony with nature through the experience of the traditional Vision Quest. Excerpts from participants' journals add an intimate dimension to this unique account of human challenge.

Building an Ark: Tools for the Preservation of Natural Diversity Through Land Protection, by Phillip M. Hoose. Illustrations. $12.00
The author is national protection planner for The Nature Conservancy, and this book presents a comprehensive plan that can be used within each state to identify and protect what remains of each area's natural ecological diversity. Case studies augment this blueprint for conservation.

Perfection Perception, with the Brothers O. and Joe de Vivre. $5.00
Notes from a metaphysical journey through the mountains of Patagonia. These two authors share their experiences and discoveries in using their powers of perception to change the world. Their thoughts are mystical at times, but their basis is firmly experiential and parallels the most theoretically advanced works in modern physics.

Please enclose $1.00 with each order for postage and handling.
California residents add 6% sales tax.
A catalog of current and forthcoming titles is available free of charge.

THIS BOOK was edited by Jeremy Hewes,
proofread by Linda Gunnarson and
designed and produced by Georgia Oliva.
The text type is Sabon, set by Michael Sykes
at Community Type & Design, Fairfax, California,
where mechanicals were prepared by Janis Gloystein.
The display type was set in Trump Medieavel
by Omnicomp, San Francisco.